Character Quotations

Activities That Build
Character and Community

D1567450

Tom Lickona & Matt Davidson

Kagan

Kagan Publishing
981 Calle Amanecer
San Clemente, CA 92673
800.933.2667
www.KaganOnline.com

ISBN: 978-1-879097-78-0

TABLE OF CONTENTS

CHARACTER QUOTATIONS
ACTIVITIES THAT BUILD CHARACTER AND COMMUNITY

"CHARACTER QUOTATIONS" **Tom Lickona and Matt Davidson**
Kagan Publishing • 1(800) 933-2667 • www.KaganOnline.com

i

Virtue Chart of Activities & Blacklines

Week	Virtue	Activities	Blacklines
1	Effort	pg. 18	pg. 20
2	Positive Attitude	pg. 26	pg. 28
3	Kindness	pg. 34	pg. 36
4	Diligence	pg. 42	pg. 44
5	Positive Attitude	pg. 50	pg. 52
6	Respect	pg. 58	pg. 60
7	Perseverance	pg. 66	pg. 68
8	Responsibility	pg. 74	pg. 76
9	Honesty	pg. 82	pg. 84
10	Gratitude	pg. 90	pg. 92
11	Work	pg. 98	pg. 100
12	Friendship	pg. 106	pg. 108
13	Forgiveness	pg. 114	pg. 116
14	Generosity	pg. 122	pg. 124
15	Cooperation	pg. 130	pg. 132
16	Confidence	pg. 138	pg. 140
17	Tolerance/Diversity	pg. 146	pg. 148
18	Justice/Fairness	pg. 154	pg. 156
19	Self-Control/Self-Discipline	pg. 162	pg. 164
20	Fortitude	pg. 170	pg. 172
21	Courage	pg. 178	pg. 180
22	Citizenship	pg. 186	pg. 188
23	Effort	pg. 194	pg. 196
24	Conscience	pg. 202	pg. 204
25	Respect	pg. 210	pg. 212
26	Perseverance	pg. 218	pg. 220
27	Cheerfulness	pg. 226	pg. 228
28	Trustworthiness	pg. 234	pg. 236
29	Reputation	pg. 242	pg. 244
30	Work	pg. 250	pg. 252
31	Kindness	pg. 258	pg. 260
32	Justice/Fairness	pg. 266	pg. 268
33	Responsibility	pg. 274	pg. 276
34	Wisdom	pg. 282	pg. 284
35	Inner Peace	pg. 290	pg. 292
36	Wisdom	pg. 298	pg. 300

"CHARACTER QUOTATIONS" Tom Lickona and Matt Davidson
Kagan Publishing • 1(800) 933-2667 • www.KaganOnline.com

Using Character Quotations to Build Character and Community

The Need for Character Education

Through history, and in cultures all over the world, education has had two great goals: to help students become smart and to help them become good. They need character for both. They need character qualities such as a strong work ethic, self-discipline, and perseverance in order to do their best in school and succeed in life. They need character qualities such as respect and responsibility in order to have positive interpersonal relationships and live in community.

Dedication

To the John Templeton Foundation, with gratitude for its support of our Center's work and its commitment to the power of wise words to build good character.

The signs of a renewed concern for character education are many: a spate of character education books and curricular materials, federal funding for character education, character education mandates in more than two-thirds of states, the emergence of national advocacy groups such as the Character Education Partnership and the Character Counts! Coalition, the appearance of university-based centers for character education (we operate one on our campus at SUNY Cortland), a *Journal of Research on Character Education*, a National Schools of Character awards competition, national reports on how to prepare future teachers to be character educators, and an explosion of grassroots character education initiatives.

The return to character education appears to be driven by several factors: (1) the weakening of the family as a moral socializer; (2) the increasing pervasiveness of the media culture as a shaper of youth values; (3) the public's perception of societal moral decline, including youth trends showing high and often rising levels of crime, bullying, incivility, cheating, materialism, substance abuse, and sexual activity; and (4) educators' realization that relativistic values education methods—ones that told students to "make your own decision" without grounding them in an understanding of the content of character—have been part of the problem.

Whatever the causes of our current social-moral problems, and regardless whether one perceives the problems as worse today than in the past, there is now widespread agreement that character education should be at the center of every school's mission. The question before schools is not whether to use character education, but rather how to do it effectively.

Using Quotations in Character Education

I can live for two months on one good compliment.
—Mark Twain
It is better to light one candle than to curse the darkness.
—proverb
Character is what you do on the third and fourth tries.
—James Michener
A single twig breaks, but a bundle of twigs is strong.
—Tecumseh

What is it about quotations like these that make them so appealing?

- They are memorable—making an important point in an original, pithy, or provocative way.
- They are enduring—expressing a timeless truth about human nature or the human condition.
- They come from many cultures—showing that wisdom transcends societal and religious diversity.
- They stimulate thought—leading us to ponder why the quote is true and how it might apply to our own experience and help us in our life.

Why are quotations like these a valuable character education resource?

- They offer insights into character—the inner strengths of mind, heart, and will that enable us to lead purposeful, productive, and fulfilling lives.
- They offer opportunities to develop moral awareness, perspective, and conscience.
- They provide a call to moral action.
- They offer wisdom from important role models.
- They provide cognitive shortcuts to complex moral concepts.
- They provide memorable maxims, which over time are continually accessible to young people and can guide their decision-making.
- They provide meaningful entry points into literary, historical, and moral content.

In this book, we have provided 180 character quotations (5 for each of 36 weeks) that we think are a good developmental match for young people in grades 3 through 8. Building on our research to promote character development in sixth-grade students,[1] we have attempted to develop a multidimensional teaching guide that can be used to foster character development in diverse educational settings, including the classroom, school, family, and youth development programs.

The Content of Character

We've chosen quotes with an eye on diversity—representing men and women, ancient sages, contemporary figures, and cultures from around the world. We've tried to cover a wide range of human virtues that nearly everyone would consider important to success in school and success in life.

We define character to include both "performance character" and "moral character." We've therefore chosen quotes that relate to: (1) virtues such as effort, work, and perseverance that make up performance character, and (2) virtues such as kindness, tolerance, and honesty that are part of moral character.

Performance character helps young people excel in their schoolwork, extra-curricular activities, and outside-of-school responsibilities. Moral character helps youth show respect and responsibility in their interpersonal relationships.

A word about terminology: Some character educators use the word "value" rather than "virtue." Some prefer "character trait" or simply "word of the week (or month)." In this book, we use the term virtue to mean a "value in action," since the ultimate measure of our character is what we actually do. However, each school has to decide what character language best fits its school and community culture.

The Organization of This Book

We've organized the quotations around a weekly virtue, such as kindness, perseverance, or honesty. For some virtues, we've provided a week's worth of quotes; for others there are two weeks' worth, at different places in the school year. Where possible, we've tried to locate a virtue at a point that fits the school calendar—gratitude near Thanksgiving, tolerance near Martin Luther King's birthday, and courage and perseverance near the birthdays of Lincoln and Washington.

The weeks generally alternate between performance character and moral character, conveying the message that we need character both to do well and to do good. We begin the school year with the performance virtue of effort—appropriate, we think, for helping each student start the year on the right foot.

The organization we've proposed, however, is only one of many possible schemes. Schools engaged in character education may have target character traits already assigned to a particular timetable and may wish to rearrange our suggested sequence of weeks. A school that focuses on perseverance for a whole month, for example, might wish to bring together four weeks of quotes dealing with that theme and related virtues, such as effort and work.

Reflection Questions on the Quotes

For each quote we've suggested at least one reflection question which can be used as a writing prompt or discussion starter. The reflection questions are meant to unpack the quote by challenging students to interact with the statement, reflecting on their own experiences and the experiences of others. Over time, opportunities to reflect on character quotations can provide students with a moral compass that will help them navigate the rapids of an often complex moral world.

Some teachers have each student keep a Character Quotes Journal in which he or she copies down the daily quote and enter reflections on it. Says one teacher who has done this, "I see kids who still have their Character Quotes Journal years later. It's something they really value." Personal written reflection on character issues provides students with significant opportunities to develop a lasting moral identity.

Different Ways to Use the Quotes

We believe that any teacher, regardless of subject area, can use character quotes to create "an environment of character" and help students become more committed to character. Some teachers simply like to display quotes—and perhaps leave certain ones posted—even if they don't have much time for writing or discussion. There is nothing wrong with this approach; simply making these concepts continually accessible to students is an important first step. Other teachers post the quotes and ask students to copy them down, taking time every so often for a brief discussion.

Chapter 2 by Miguel Kagan describes how to use various cooperative learning structures to create focused and productive discussion of the quotes, weekly virtues, and the general concept of character. Structures such as Timed-Pair-Share, Team Statements, and Jigsaw will help spark lively exchanges among students.

Moving from Awareness to Action

Teachers who want to get the most developmental mileage out of a quote must look for ways to help students internalize and act upon it. As a character development strategy, quotations are most effective when they move students from awareness to action—when they influence the choices they make in their own lives.

"CHARACTER QUOTATIONS" Tom Lickona and Matt Davidson
Kagan Publishing • 1(800) 933-2667 • www.KaganOnline.com

Toward that end we've provided weekly "action assignments"—varied activities that help each student make the lesson of a quote part of his or her personal character. Many of these activities challenge students to set goals and assess their progress toward attaining them. These assignments are intended to bring home the idea that character development is not a spectator sport. Some sample assignments include:

- **Positive Attitude**—Find and interview a person who shows a positive attitude. Ask that person, "How do you keep a positive attitude, even when things go wrong? How does a positive attitude help you?"

- **Fortitude**—Make a list of things that are particularly difficult or challenging for you. Choose one and make a plan for meeting that challenge. Share your plan with a partner.

- **Generosity**—Put everybody's name in a hat. The name in your class you draw is your "secret pal" for that week. As a class, generate a list of nice things you could do for your "secret pal." Each day do something nice without your pal knowing it was you.

- **Responsibility**—As a class, select and discuss a classroom, school, or community problem that the class might help to solve. Make an action plan and carry it out.

- **Forgiveness**—Write about a time when somebody forgave you; describe how you felt. As a class, discuss, "What feelings often make it hard for us to forgive another? What are some things we can do to overcome those feelings?" Decide as a class how you will "let bygones be bygones."

Character education is sometimes criticized as "being a mile wide and an inch deep." Posters, slogans, and even good quotes can be used superficially in a way that may be dismissed as "bumper sticker morality."

Action assignments, however, go a long way toward ensuring that character education is truly transformative. In combination with the content of the character quotes and reflection questions, weekly assignments that require students to engage in deliberate moral action have the potential to: (a) develop the three parts of individual character (knowing the good, desiring the good, and doing the good), and (b) develop the character of the classroom and school.

When students, individually or as a class, plan and carry out ways to act upon a virtue, character comes to life in the culture of the school community. Therefore, we strongly encourage educators to use these character quotes in a way that engages each student in meaningful action that can make a difference in the person he or she is becoming.

Creating a Character Quotation Bulletin Board

This book was designed to facilitate the creation of a character quotation bulletin board. The bulletin board consists of two sections corresponding to the two types of pages included for each virtue: 1) Virtue of the Week, and 2) Quotes of the Day.

Virtue of the Week

For the virtue of the week, copy the last reproducible page of the virtue. This page has the name of the virtue in large print and an illustration representing the virtue.

Quotes of the Day

This section consists of the five preceding reproducible quotes, one for each day of the week.

The bulletin board can be created at the beginning of the week, or it can be constructed throughout the week, with each quote added daily after it is presented to the class. Each quote may also be copied onto a transparency and shown on an overhead projector.

Comprehensive Character Education

Character quotes will have their greatest effect when they are one of many strategies in a comprehensive approach. A comprehensive approach includes character-rich literature, ongoing ethical reflection, cooperative learning, discipline that promotes moral understanding, class meetings, conflict resolution, service learning, a challenging academic program, and a total school environment that upholds and reinforces the school's professed character virtues. Many of the strategies that make up a comprehensive approach—such as ethical reflection, cooperative learning, class meetings, and service learning—are in fact integrated into this book's reflection questions, discussion activities, and action assignments.

The Enduring Power of Quotes

Research suggests the power of quotations can become guiding motivational principles in the lives of young people. One university student reported that the maxim, *"A stitch in time saves nine,"* had been his guiding principle since the age of nine. The maxim impressed him so much that he integrated it into his life, thinks about it daily, and finds a way to apply it to most situations. The maxim has been a mechanism for helping him to remain focused on his goals and doing what was necessary in order to achieve them.[2]

Most of us chose education as our field of work because we wanted to touch a child's life in a lasting way. Teaching wisdom is one good way to do that. For each of the authors of this book, the wisdom of particular quotes has stood the test of time. Matt remembers Coach Hugh Moyer saying, *"It's not enough to stare up the steps, you've got to step up the stairs"*; and his mom saying, *"Smile, and the whole world smiles with you; frown, and you frown alone."* Tom remembers a college teacher who offered this quote as a defense against discouragement: *"Two men looked through the prison bars. One saw mud, and the other saw stars."*

Wise words are food for the soul. We cheat our students if we don't give them many opportunities to encounter and grapple with what thoughtful people have said about what it means to be a person of character and to live life well.

Tom Lickona and Matt Davidson
Cortland, New York

Endnotes

1. Davidson, M.L., (2000). *Using moral maxims to promote character development in sixth-grade students.* Unpublished Dissertation. Ithaca, NY: Cornell University.

2. Prahlad, A.D.F., (1994). "No guts, no glory" *Proverbs, values, and image among Anglo-American university students. Southern Folklore,* 51, 285–298.

"CHARACTER QUOTATIONS" Tom Lickona and Matt Davidson
Kagan Publishing • 1(800) 933-2667 • www.KaganOnline.com

Using Cooperative Structures to Discuss Quotations, Virtues, and the Concept of Character

by Miguel Kagan

The process by which students interact with the content of the character quotes is nearly as important as the content itself. What students remember and actually put into practice will depend largely on how they come to know and internalize the wisdom of the quotes. This chapter shows how to use seven different cooperative learning structures to *actively engage* students in the examination and development of character. These activities are categorized into three types:

Quote of the Day
Activities focusing on the daily quote. Activities can be in place of, or in addition to, the daily Reflection Questions.

Virtue of the Week
These activities expand on the featured virtue. They are intended as additional avenues for students to actively explore the selected virtue together.

Spotlight on Character
Character itself comes into the spotlight. Students discuss and develop their concept of character and its importance.

Some of the cooperative structures will work well for all three activity types.

Timed-Pair-Share

Virtue of the Week

The teacher asks a question, either pertaining to the virtue of the week or to all of that week's daily quotes taken together.

For example:

- *Of the five quotes, which one appeals to you most? Why?*
- *Who do you know that is a good role model for this week's virtue? Describe that person.*

Students silently think for a while about how they would answer the question. Students pair up. Partner A shares his or her response for a predetermined amount of time. Partner B shares for the same amount of time.

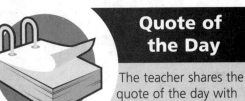

Quote of the Day

The teacher shares the quote of the day with the class and asks students a question related to the quote. Each quote of the day (see Chapter 3) has at least one associated Reflection Question that can be used for journaling and/or interactive discussion. For example, during Week 2 on Attitude, one of the daily quotes is, *"Your attitude determines your altitude."* A recommended Reflection Question is, "How does having a positive attitude help you to do your best?" The teacher gives students time to think and formulate their responses to the Reflection Question. Students then pair up. Partner A shares his or her response for one minute (or any predetermined amount of time). Then Partner B shares for the same amount of time.

In addition to the suggested quote-specific Reflection Questions in Chapter 3, here are a few generic questions the teacher might also ask:

- *What is this quote telling us?*
- *Why is this true?*
- *Why is this important?*

Spotlight on Character

Timed-Pair-Share is also a good format for discussing virtues and character in general. The teacher can post quotes from different weeks, compare virtues, or ask more general questions about character.

For example:

- *Of these three virtues, which is most important for people to acquire? Why?*
- *What is the difference between effort and perseverance?*
- *Why does following our conscience sometimes require courage?*
- *Why is it important to have good character?*

Students reflect on how they would answer. They pair up and take turns responding, each for the allotted time.

"CHARACTER QUOTATIONS" Tom Lickona and Matt Davidson
Kagan Publishing • 1(800) 933-2667 • www.KaganOnline.com

Corners

Spotlight on Character

The teacher chooses four different virtues and posts the name of a virtue in each corner of the room. The teacher reads the four virtues and asks an open-ended question that has students choose a virtue and go to that corner.

For example:

- *Of the four virtues, which is the most important attribute for the President to have?*
- *Which of the four virtues is least common to find in people today?*
- *If you could strengthen one of the four virtues in yourself, which would it be?*
- *Which of the four virtues are you most proud of having? Why?*

Students think about the question and record their corner selection. They leave their seats and go to their chosen corner. In their corners, pairs discuss the answer to the question and why they chose the corner they did. After students discuss with a partner from their own corner, they pair up with a partner from a different corner to hear a different perspective.

Virtue of the Week

The teacher posts four quotes on the same virtue in the four corners of the room. The teacher reads the four quotes aloud to students and asks a question that requires students to select one of the four corners.

For example:

- *Of the four quotes, which one best captures the essence of cooperation?*
- *If you had to select one of the four quotes as your personal motto, which would it be?*

After thinking, each student writes down his or her corner selection on a slip of paper; then moves to that corner. In the corners, students pair up and discuss with their partner why they chose that corner.

The teacher then calls on students from each corner to share their ideas with the class. To ensure listening and comprehension, students from other corners may be asked to paraphrase their responses. (If no student chooses a particular corner, the teacher may go there and comment on that quote.)

"CHARACTER QUOTATIONS" **Tom Lickona and Matt Davidson**
Kagan Publishing • 1(800) 933-2667 • www.KaganOnline.com

11

Character is...

Team Statements

Virtue of the Week

The teacher assigns the virtue of the week. Each team's task is to write a brief statement summarizing the essence of cooperation. Suppose the virtue is "cooperation." They start their statement with, "Cooperation is..." The team statement should be a concise statement that captures the essence of the virtue. For example, the team may come up with, "Many heads are better than one." Once they reach consensus on the team's statement, teammates write the statement on a designated area of the board, or they read it in unison to their classmates.

Quote of the Day

Each team has the task of writing a brief statement responding to the Reflection Question for the quote of the day. (Most of Chapter 3's Reflection Questions, such as "What does this quote mean?", lend themselves to a team response.) First, students independently write their own statements. Teammates take turns sharing their statements. After all individual statements are read, team members put their heads together to synthesize the individual statements into a team statement.

Spotlight on Character

Teams come up with a Team Statement on character. Here are some possible statement starters:

- *Character is...*
- *A virtue is...*
- *A virtuous person is...*
- *Character matters because...*
- *A positive role model is...*

"CHARACTER QUOTATIONS" Tom Lickona and Matt Davidson
Kagan Publishing • 1(800) 933-2667 • www.KaganOnline.com

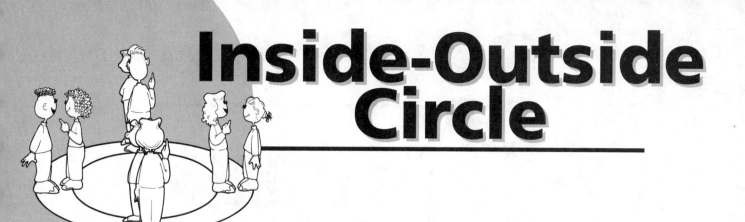

Inside-Outside Circle

Spotlight on Character

Each student receives a quote of the day. Students pair up, so there is an A and a B partner. All the A's form a large circle in the classroom. All the B's move inside the circle to face their partners. The result is two concentric circles of students, an inside circle (B's) and an outside circle (A's).

The teacher tells the class that they will do a Timed-Pair-Share. The A Partners read their quotes to the B Partners, and then have 30 seconds to explain what their quotes mean. After the thirty seconds, B Partners thank A Partners for their explanation. Then it's B Partners' turn: They have 30 seconds to read their quotes to the A Partners and explain what it means. After both partners have shared, they trade quotes and say goodbye.

The teacher then calls out a rotation number, for example, "Inside circle, rotate three partners clockwise." Students are now facing a new partner. They repeat the Timed-Pair-Share, this time sharing and interpreting the new quote.

RallyRobin

Virtue of the Week

Students pair up. The teacher gives pairs a question or sentence starter related to the virtue of the week. Partners take turns coming up with as many answers as possible.

For example:

- *Responsibility means...*
- *Responsibility is important because...*
- *We show responsibility by...*

Spotlight on Character

Students form pairs. The teacher gives pairs a question or prompt to which there are many possible answers.

For example:

- *Name a profession and a virtue associated with that profession.*
- *Why is character important? List the reasons.*
- *Which virtues do you appreciate when you encounter them in others? (For example, "I appreciate it when people are kind to me and others.")*

In pairs, students take turns coming up with answers.

❝CHARACTER QUOTATIONS❞ Tom Lickona and Matt Davidson
Kagan Publishing • 1(800) 933-2667 • www.KaganOnline.com

Jigsaw

Virtue of the Week

In a team of four, each student receives a different quote of the day on the virtue of the week. The teacher posts the four quotes in the four corners of the room and announces the corners to students. Students stand up and go to the corner with their quote.

In their corners, students pair up to discuss their quote—either answering the quote-specific Reflection Question or another question of the teacher's choosing. The goal is to report and explain their answer to the teammates when they return.

In their corners, pairs discuss how they can best present their answer to their teammates. Alternative presentation modes include drawing, acting, poems, raps, and skits. Students return to their teams. They take turns presenting.

Spotlight on Character

In a team of four, each student is assigned a different virtue. The teacher posts the four virtues in the four corners of the room and announces the corners to students. Students stand up and go to the corner with their virtue. In their corners, students pair up. Pairs work together to prepare how they can independently best teach their teammates about the virtue. The pair can:

- *Write a definition of the virtue.*
- *Create a song or poem about the virtue.*
- *Draw a picture showing the virtue being practiced.*
- *Orchestrate a pantomime.*

Students return to their teams. They take turns presenting.

Journal Reflections

Virtue of the Week

Here are some general writing prompts that work with any virtue of the week:

- *Define the virtue in your own words.*
- *How does this virtue affect others?*
- *What are the advantages of possessing this virtue?*
- *Which quote holds the most truth for you?*
- *Compare and contrast any two quotes of the day on this virtue.*
- *What does each of the daily quotes tell us about this virtue—how does each one add to our understanding?*
- *What general rule could you state based on the quotes about this virtue?*
- *Name a time in your life when you did something to display this virtue. How did it make you feel?*
- *Write a short story illustrating this virtue in action.*
- *Write a brief dialogue about this virtue.*
- *Write a poem about this virtue.*
- *Draw a picture illustrating this virtue.*

Quote of the Day

The teacher presents the quote of the day to the class. Using the suggested Reflection Question(s) (Chapter 3), students first discuss the quote, and then write their thoughts in a Character Quotes Journal. Alternatively, they can write first in response to the question and then share their journal entry with a partner or small group.

In addition to the quote-specific Reflection Questions, here are some generic journal writing topics:

- *What does this quote make you think about? Write anything that comes to mind.*
- *What does this quote mean?*
- *Can you give an example from your life that illustrates the importance of this quote?*
- *What is the author of this quote saying about the virtue?*
- *Write the opposite of this quote and explain why the opposite is not true.*
- *If you were going to explain this quote to a younger person, what would you say?*
- *Write a short story illustrating this quote.*
- *If you made this quote your personal motto, what would you do differently in your life?*

Spotlight on Character

Here are some of the many possibilities for journal writing on the general theme of character:

- *Describe a person of good character.*
- *What three character virtues do you think everyone should have and why?*
- *Think of a person in history that you admire. Describe the virtue(s) this person possessed.*
- *Write a short story about one of your heroes or heroines and the character qualities that person has.*
- *How are you like and unlike your hero or heroine?*
- *List the five virtues that are most important in your life. Explain why these are important for you.*
- *How do we develop our character?*
- *What major events in your life have influenced your character?*
- *What are two steps you could take, beginning now, to improve your character?*

"CHARACTER QUOTATIONS" Tom Lickona and Matt Davidson
Kagan Publishing • 1(800) 933-2667 • www.KaganOnline.com

Chapter 3

Weekly Character Quotations, Reflection Questions, and Action Assignments

EFFORT

THE DELIBERATE EXERTION OF MENTAL OR PHYSICAL POWER.

WEEK 1

TUESDAY

2

A teacher opens the door, but you must enter yourself.
—**Chinese proverb**

Reflection Question
- *What does this mean? (Put it in your own words.)*

MONDAY

1

Character is not inherited. One builds it daily by the way one thinks and acts, thought by thought, action by action.
—**Helen Gahagan Douglas**

Reflection Questions
- *Are you born with good character, or is it something you have to work on?*

- *What are two ways you can develop your character?*

ACTION ASSIGNMENTS

- List three of your positive character traits.

- Identify one character trait you need to work on. Make a plan to improve it.

- At the end of each day, reflect on how well you followed your plan for improvement (e.g., keep a journal).

There's no easy way to learn difficult things.

—Joseph de Maistre

Reflection Questions
- *What is something that was hard for you to learn?*

- *How did you learn it?*

You may be disappointed if you fail, but you are doomed if you don't try.

—Beverly Sills

Reflection Question
- *What keeps you from trying something you're not good at?*

The journey of a thousand miles begins with a single step.

—Lao-tzu

Reflection Question
- *What is a personal journey that you have begun?*

"CHARACTER QUOTATIONS" Tom Lickona and Matt Davidson
Kagan Publishing • 1(800) 933-2667 • www.KaganOnline.com

EFFORT

Character is not inherited. One builds it daily by the way one thinks and acts, thought by thought, action by action.

—Helen Gahagan Douglas

Effort

EFFORT

A teacher opens the door, but you must enter yourself.

—Chinese proverb

EFFORT

There's no easy way to learn difficult things.

—Joseph de Maistre

Effort

"CHARACTER QUOTATIONS" Tom Lickona and Matt Davidson
Kagan Publishing • 1(800) 933-2667 • www.KaganOnline.com

EFFORT

You may be disappointed if you fail, but you are doomed if you don't try.

—Beverly Sills

"CHARACTER QUOTATIONS" Tom Lickona and Matt Davidson
Kagan Publishing • 1(800) 933-2667 • www.KaganOnline.com

EFFORT

The journey of a thousand miles begins with a single step.

—Lao-tzu

Effort

"CHARACTER QUOTATIONS" Tom Lickona and Matt Davidson
Kagan Publishing • 1(800) 933-2667 • www.KaganOnline.com

EFFORT

“CHARACTER QUOTATIONS” Tom Lickona and Matt Davidson
Kagan Publishing • 1(800) 933-2667 • www.KaganOnline.com

POSITIVE ATTITUDE

A CONFIDENT OR OPTIMISTIC STATE OF MIND.

WEEK 2

2 *TUESDAY*

Your attitude determines your altitude.

—Jesse Jackson

Reflection Questions

• *How does having a positive attitude help you to do your best?*

• *How does having a bad attitude keep you from doing your best?*

1 *MONDAY*

Sow a thought, and you reap an act. Sow an act, and you reap a habit. Sow a habit, and you reap a character.

—William Makepeace Thackery

Reflection Questions

• *What does it mean to sow and reap?*

• *What does it mean to say, "Our habits become our character?"*

ACTION ASSIGNMENTS

• Find and interview a person who shows a positive attitude. Ask the person two questions: "How do you keep a positive attitude, even when things go wrong?" "How does a positive attitude help you?"

• Each day, keep track of the number of times you complain (about anything). Each day, try to reduce the number of your complaints (continuing to keep track).

WEDNESDAY

Each new hour holds chances for new beginnings.
—Maya Angelou

Reflection Questions
- *When something goes wrong, why is it important for you to make a new start?*

- *What happens if you let one mistake or bad experience get you down?*

THURSDAY

I am convinced that life is 10% what happens to me and 90% how I react to it. And so it is with you. We are in charge of our attitudes.
—Charles Swindoll

Reflection Questions
- *When is a time that keeping a positive attitude helped you overcome a difficult situation?*

- *What can you do to keep a positive attitude when things become difficult?*

FRIDAY

Hold fast to dreams, for if dreams die, life is a broken-winged bird that cannot fly.
—Langston Hughes

Reflection Questions
- *What is something you dream of doing or becoming?*

- *How does having a goal or dream give us energy, purpose, and direction?*

"CHARACTER QUOTATIONS" Tom Lickona and Matt Davidson
Kagan Publishing • 1(800) 933-2667 • www.KaganOnline.com

POSITIVE ATTITUDE

Sow a thought and you reap an act. Sow an act and you reap a habit. Sow a habit and you reap a character.

—William Makepeace Thackery

Positive Attitude

POSITIVE ATTITUDE

Your attitude determines your altitude.

—Jesse Jackson

"CHARACTER QUOTATIONS" Tom Lickona and Matt Davidson
Kagan Publishing • 1(800) 933-2667 • www.KaganOnline.com

POSITIVE ATTITUDE

Each new hour holds chances for new beginnings.

—Maya Angelou

Positive Attitude

"CHARACTER QUOTATIONS" Tom Lickona and Matt Davidson
Kagan Publishing • 1(800) 933-2667 • www.KaganOnline.com

POSITIVE ATTITUDE

I am convinced that life is 10% what happens to me and 90% how I react to it. And so it is with you. We are in charge of our attitudes.

—Charles Swindoll

"CHARACTER QUOTATIONS" Tom Lickona and Matt Davidson
Kagan Publishing • 1(800) 933-2667 • www.KaganOnline.com

POSITIVE ATTITUDE

Hold fast to dreams, for if dreams die, life is a broken-winged bird that cannot fly.

—Langston Hughes

"CHARACTER QUOTATIONS" Tom Lickona and Matt Davidson
Kagan Publishing • 1(800) 933-2667 • www.KaganOnline.com

POSITIVE ATTITUDE

“CHARACTER QUOTATIONS” Tom Lickona and Matt Davidson
Kagan Publishing • 1(800) 933-2667 • www.KaganOnline.com

KINDNESS

THE QUALITY OF BEING
CONSIDERATE OR HELPFUL.

WEEK 3

TUESDAY

2

I can live for two months on one good compliment.

—Mark Twain

Reflection Questions
* *Why do compliments make us feel so good?*

* *If compliments make everyone feel so good, why don't we give them more often?*

MONDAY

1

No one who desires to become good will become good without doing good things.

—Aristotle

Reflection Question
* *What can you do to become more considerate and helpful toward others?*

ACTION ASSIGNMENTS

* Interview an adult; ask, "What can you do to become a good person?"

* Set a goal to compliment at least five people today. (Keep track.)

* During this week, do a kind deed each day for someone in your classroom, school, family, or neighborhood.

34

Sticks and stones may break our bones, but words will break our hearts.

—Robert Fulghum

Reflection Questions
- *Why do words often hurt more than a physical injury?*

- *What can you do if you hear someone saying hurtful words to another person?*

Kindness gives birth to kindness.

—Sophocles

Reflection Question
- *How might one act of kindness lead to more kindness from others?*

You cannot do a kindness too soon, for you never know how soon it will be too late.

—Ralph Waldo Emerson

Reflection Question
- *What does this mean?*

"CHARACTER QUOTATIONS" Tom Lickona and Matt Davidson
Kagan Publishing • 1(800) 933-2667 • www.KaganOnline.com

KINDNESS

No one who desires to become good will become good without doing good things.

—Aristotle

Kindness

"CHARACTER QUOTATIONS" Tom Lickona and Matt Davidson
Kagan Publishing • 1(800) 933-2667 • www.KaganOnline.com

KINDNESS

I can live for two months on one good compliment.

—Mark Twain

"CHARACTER QUOTATIONS" Tom Lickona and Matt Davidson
Kagan Publishing • 1(800) 933-2667 • www.KaganOnline.com

KINDNESS

Sticks and stones may break our bones, but words will break our hearts.

—Robert Fulghum

Kindness

"CHARACTER QUOTATIONS" Tom Lickona and Matt Davidson
Kagan Publishing • 1(800) 933-2667 • www.KaganOnline.com

KINDNESS

Kindness gives birth to kindness.

—Sophocles

Kindness

"CHARACTER QUOTATIONS" Tom Lickona and Matt Davidson
Kagan Publishing • 1(800) 933-2667 • www.KaganOnline.com

KINDNESS

You cannot do a kindness too soon, for you never know how soon it will be too late.

—Ralph Waldo Emerson

"CHARACTER QUOTATIONS" Tom Lickona and Matt Davidson
Kagan Publishing • 1(800) 933-2667 • www.KaganOnline.com

KINDNESS

“CHARACTER QUOTATIONS” Tom Lickona and Matt Davidson
Kagan Publishing • 1(800) 933-2667 • www.KaganOnline.com

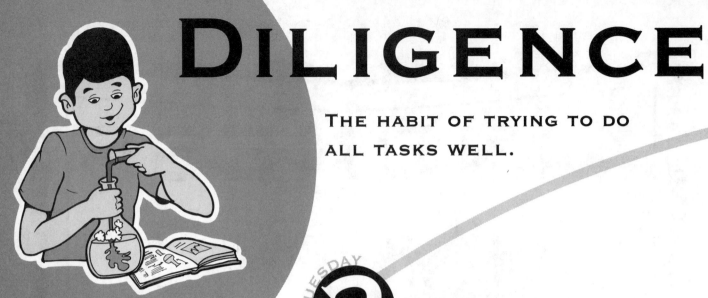

DILIGENCE

THE HABIT OF TRYING TO DO ALL TASKS WELL.

WEEK 4

TUESDAY

2

Learning is not attained by chance. It must be sought for with ardor and attended to with diligence.

—Abigail Adams

Reflection Question
- *Why is it easier to learn something if you have an enthusiastic attitude?*

MONDAY

1

Excellence is not an act but a habit.

—Aristotle

Reflection Question
- *What does this quote mean? (Put it on your own words.)*

ACTION ASSIGNMENTS

- What is at least one thing you could do to improve your work in school? Ask a teacher and an adult in your home for additional suggestions.

- Interview a person who is really good at something. Ask, "How did you become good at this?"

WEDNESDAY

Any job worth doing is worth doing well.

—proverb

Reflection Question
• *Why is it important to try your hardest to do a job well?*

THURSDAY

The secret joy in work is excellence. To know how to do something well is to enjoy it.

—Pearl Buck

Reflection Question
• *When was a time that you felt good because you did a job well?*

FRIDAY

The best preparation for tomorrow is to do today's work superbly well.

—William Osler

Reflection Question
• *How does what we do today prepare us for tomorrow?*

Diligence

"CHARACTER QUOTATIONS" Tom Lickona and Matt Davidson
Kagan Publishing • 1(800) 933-2667 • www.KaganOnline.com

DILIGENCE

Excellence is not an act but a habit.

—Aristotle

"CHARACTER QUOTATIONS" Tom Lickona and Matt Davidson
Kagan Publishing • 1(800) 933-2667 • www.KaganOnline.com

DILIGENCE

Learning is not attained by chance. It must be sought for with ardor and attended to with diligence.

—Abigail Adams

"CHARACTER QUOTATIONS" **Tom Lickona and Matt Davidson**
Kagan Publishing • 1(800) 933-2667 • www.KaganOnline.com

DILIGENCE

Any job worth doing is worth doing well.

—proverb

"CHARACTER QUOTATIONS" Tom Lickona and Matt Davidson
Kagan Publishing • 1(800) 933-2667 • www.KaganOnline.com

DILIGENCE

The secret joy in work is excellence. To know how to do something well is to enjoy it.

—Pearl Buck

Diligence

"CHARACTER QUOTATIONS" Tom Lickona and Matt Davidson
Kagan Publishing • 1(800) 933-2667 • www.KaganOnline.com

DILIGENCE

The best preparation for tomorrow is to do today's work superbly well.

—William Osler

"CHARACTER QUOTATIONS" Tom Lickona and Matt Davidson
Kagan Publishing • 1(800) 933-2667 • www.KaganOnline.com

DILIGENCE

“CHARACTER QUOTATIONS” Tom Lickona and Matt Davidson
Kagan Publishing • 1(800) 933-2667 • www.KaganOnline.com

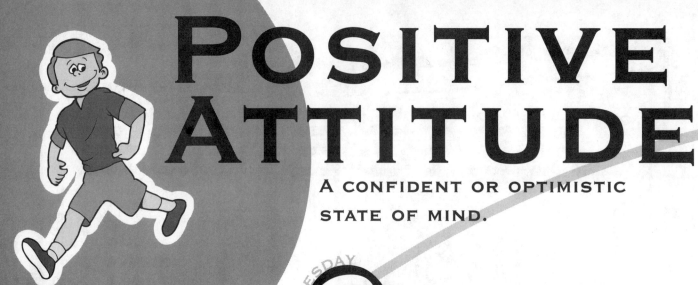

POSITIVE ATTITUDE

A CONFIDENT OR OPTIMISTIC STATE OF MIND.

WEEK 5

TUESDAY

2

Most people are about as happy as they make up their minds to be.

—Abraham Lincoln

Reflection Question

- *What are some things we can do to help ourselves have positive attitudes?*

MONDAY

1

Every problem is an opportunity in disguise.

—proverb

Reflection Questions

- *What does this mean? (Put it in your own words.)*

- *What is a problem you're having now that you could turn into an opportunity?*

ACTION ASSIGNMENTS

- Think of something that you really don't like to do. List some things you could do to help yourself have a better attitude when doing this.

- Try to go one whole day without complaining about anything. (If you slip, don't quit. Keep trying! If you complain about something, write down what it was.)

3

If you don't like something, change it. If you can't change it, change your attitude. Don't complain.
—Maya Angelou

Reflection Questions
- *Why does complaining about something usually make us feel worse instead of better?*

- *How does our complaining affect those around us?*

4

I am determined to be cheerful and happy in whatever situation I may be. For I have learned from experience that the greater part of our happiness or misery depends on our dispositions [attitudes] and not on our circumstances.
—Martha Washington

Reflection Question
- *When was a time in your life that you kept a positive attitude in an uncomfortable or difficult situation?*

5

Everything can be taken from us except one thing— the freedom to choose our attitude in any set of circumstances.

—Viktor Frankl
(Nazi concentration camp survivor)

Reflection Questions
- *How could this thought help Viktor Frankl and other persons in difficult situations keep a positive attitude?*

- *How could you use this quote to help yourself keep a positive attitude during difficult times?*

POSITIVE ATTITUDE

Every problem is an opportunity in disguise.

—proverb

Positive Attitude

POSITIVE ATTITUDE

Most people are about as happy as they make up their minds to be.

—Abraham Lincoln

"CHARACTER QUOTATIONS" Tom Lickona and Matt Davidson
Kagan Publishing • 1(800) 933-2667 • www.KaganOnline.com

POSITIVE ATTITUDE

If you don't like something, change it. If you can't change it, change your attitude. Don't complain.

—Maya Angelou

"CHARACTER QUOTATIONS" Tom Lickona and Matt Davidson
Kagan Publishing • 1(800) 933-2667 • www.KaganOnline.com

POSITIVE ATTITUDE

I am determined to be cheerful and happy in whatever situation I may be. For I have learned from experience that the greater part of our happiness or misery depends on our dispositions [attitudes] and not on our circumstances.

—Martha Washington

"CHARACTER QUOTATIONS" Tom Lickona and Matt Davidson
Kagan Publishing • 1(800) 933-2667 • www.KaganOnline.com

POSITIVE ATTITUDE

Everything can be taken from us except one thing— the freedom to choose our attitude in any set of circumstances.

—Viktor Frankl (Nazi concentration camp survivor)

"CHARACTER QUOTATIONS" **Tom Lickona and Matt Davidson**
Kagan Publishing • 1(800) 933-2667 • www.KaganOnline.com

POSITIVE ATTITUDE

"CHARACTER QUOTATIONS" Tom Lickona and Matt Davidson
Kagan Publishing • 1(800) 933-2667 • www.KaganOnline.com

RESPECT

WEEK 6

TUESDAY

2

If you want respect, show it.
—anonymous

Reflection Questions
- *Why is this good advice?*

- *What are two ways you can show respect for other people?*

MONDAY

1

When we do good things, our self-respect grows.
—Abraham Heschel

Reflection Question
- *When was a time that you gained self-respect because you did the right thing?*

ACTION ASSIGNMENTS

- As a class, make a list of ways that people can show respect for each other. Make another list of ways that people sometimes show disrespect towards others.

- Together, develop three or four rules that will help class members respect one another. Agree on fair and reasonable consequences for breaking any of the rules.

The strong shall not hurt the weak.

—Code of Hammurabi

Reflection Question
- *Why is this an important moral rule?*

Don't judge a book by its cover.

—maxim

Reflection Question
- *Why do people sometimes judge another person by his or her "cover"?*

That you might retain your self-respect, it is better to displease people by doing what you know is right, than to temporarily please them by doing what you know is wrong.

—William Boetcker

Reflection Questions
- *Why is it important to keep your self-respect?*

- *What is an example of a situation where it would be better to displease someone than to do what you know is wrong?*

RESPECT

When we do good things, our self-respect grows.

—Abraham Heschel

"CHARACTER QUOTATIONS" Tom Lickona and Matt Davidson
Kagan Publishing • 1(800) 933-2667 • www.KaganOnline.com

RESPECT

If you want respect, show it.

—anonymous

RESPECT

The strong shall not hurt the weak.

—Code of Hammurabi

"CHARACTER QUOTATIONS" Tom Lickona and Matt Davidson
Kagan Publishing • 1(800) 933-2667 • www.KaganOnline.com

RESPECT

Don't judge a book by its cover.

—maxim

RESPECT

That you might retain your self-respect, it is better to displease people by doing what you know is right, than to temporarily please them by doing what you know is wrong.

—William Boetcker

Respect

"CHARACTER QUOTATIONS" Tom Lickona and Matt Davidson
Kagan Publishing • 1(800) 933-2667 • www.KaganOnline.com

RESPECT

PERSEVERANCE

THE QUALITY OF PERSISTING DESPITE DIFFICULTIES.

WEEK 7

TUESDAY

2

Press on. Nothing in the world can take the place of persistence.

—Ray Kroc
(founder of McDonald's)

Reflection Question
• *Is this true? Explain.*

MONDAY

1

Character is what you do on the third and fourth tries.

—James Michener

Reflection Question
• *Why is perseverance an important part of character?*

ACTION ASSIGNMENTS

• Read the book, *The Little Engine That Could* (a story enjoyed by people of all ages) to a younger child or group of children and discuss the importance of perseverance.

• Choose something that you've struggled with or failed at. Make a plan for persevering until you succeed.

If at first you don't succeed, try, try again.

—maxim

Reflection Question
- *When was a time that you didn't succeed at first, but later succeeded because you kept trying?*

There is no such thing as failure. There is only giving up too soon.

—Jonas Salk (discoverer of the vaccine to prevent polio)

Reflection Question
- *What advice could you give to a person who failed at something to help them not give up?*

Where there's a will, there's a way.

—maxim

Reflection Question
- *What does this mean? (Put it in your own words.)*

PERSEVERANCE

Character is what you do on the third and fourth tries.

—James Michener

Perseverance

"CHARACTER QUOTATIONS" Tom Lickona and Matt Davidson
Kagan Publishing • 1(800) 933-2667 • www.KaganOnline.com

PERSEVERANCE

Press on. Nothing in the world can take the place of persistence.

**—Ray Kroc
(founder of McDonald's)**

Perseverance

"CHARACTER QUOTATIONS" Tom Lickona and Matt Davidson
Kagan Publishing • 1(800) 933-2667 • www.KaganOnline.com

PERSEVERANCE

If at first you don't succeed, try, try again.

—maxim

"CHARACTER QUOTATIONS" Tom Lickona and Matt Davidson
Kagan Publishing • 1(800) 933-2667 • www.KaganOnline.com

PERSEVERANCE

There is no such thing as failure. There is only giving up too soon.

**—Jonas Salk
(discoverer of the
vaccine to prevent polio)**

Perseverance

PERSEVERANCE

Where there's a will, there's a way.

—maxim

"CHARACTER QUOTATIONS" Tom Lickona and Matt Davidson
Kagan Publishing • 1(800) 933-2667 • www.KaganOnline.com

PERSEVERANCE

RESPONSIBILITY

ACCOUNTABILITY FOR ONE'S
ACTIONS; DEPENDABILITY.

WEEK 8

TUESDAY

2

Hold yourself responsible for a higher standard than anybody expects of you. Never excuse yourself.

—Henry Ward Beecher

Reflection Questions
- *How do we benefit when we expect more of ourselves than others expect of us?*

- *Why is it important not to make excuses when we fail to do what we know we should do?*

MONDAY

1

True freedom is not doing what we want to do, but doing what we ought to do.

—Pope John Paul II

Reflection Question
- *What does this mean? (Put it in your own words.)*

ACTION ASSIGNMENTS

- Make a list of your responsibilities at school and at home. Choose two responsibilities that you could do a better job on. Make a plan for improving on these, starting today.

- As a class, select and discuss a classroom, school, or community problem that the class might help to solve. Make an action plan and carry it out.

3

If you want rights,
Then listen to me
You gotta have responsibility.
Do your part
And you will be
A dependable part of the community.
If you said you would,
Then do it.
Got a job to do? Get to it.

—**school song**

Reflection Question

• *What happens if everyone doesn't "do his or her part" to make a good classroom, school, or community?*

4

If you're not part of the solution, you're part of the problem.

—**maxim**

Reflection Question

• *How does this apply to the problem of bullying?*

5

It is better to light one candle than to curse the darkness.

—**proverb**

Reflection Questions

• *What does this mean? (Put it in your own words.)*

• *When was a time that you took responsibility for doing something to make a situation better?*

RESPONSIBILITY

True freedom is not doing what we want to do, but doing what we ought to do.

—Pope John Paul II

RESPONSIBILITY

Hold yourself responsible for a higher standard than anybody expects of you. Never excuse yourself.

—Henry Ward Beecher

Responsibility

"CHARACTER QUOTATIONS" Tom Lickona and Matt Davidson
Kagan Publishing • 1(800) 933-2667 • www.KaganOnline.com

RESPONSIBILITY

If you want rights,
Then listen to me
You gotta have responsibility.
Do your part
And you will be
A dependable part of the community.
If you said you would,
Then do it.

Got a job to do? Get to it.

—school song

"CHARACTER QUOTATIONS" Tom Lickona and Matt Davidson
Kagan Publishing • 1(800) 933-2667 • www.KaganOnline.com

RESPONSIBILITY

If you're not part of the solution, you're part of the problem.

—maxim

"CHARACTER QUOTATIONS" Tom Lickona and Matt Davidson
Kagan Publishing • 1(800) 933-2667 • www.KaganOnline.com

RESPONSIBILITY

It is better to light one candle than to curse the darkness.

—proverb

Responsibility

"CHARACTER QUOTATIONS" Tom Lickona and Matt Davidson
Kagan Publishing • 1(800) 933-2667 • www.KaganOnline.com

RESPONSIBILITY

"CHARACTER QUOTATIONS" Tom Lickona and Matt Davidson
Kagan Publishing • 1(800) 933-2667 • www.KaganOnline.com

HONESTY

BEING TRUTHFUL; NOT
CHEATING; NOT STEALING.

WEEK 9

TUESDAY

2

Honesty is the best policy.
—Miguel de Cervantes

Reflection Questions
- *Why is this true?*

- *How can you help yourself be honest when you are tempted to be dishonest?*

MONDAY

1

Character is what you do when nobody's looking.
—J.C. Watts

Reflection Question
- *What does this mean? (Put it in your own words.)*

ACTION ASSIGNMENTS

- Read *The Boy Who Cried Wolf* to a younger child or group of children and discuss the importance of telling the truth.

- Interview your parent or another adult at home about the importance of honesty. Ask, "How will telling lies cause problems for a person, now and in the future?"

3

WEDNESDAY

Liars are not believed when they speak the truth.

—proverb

Reflection Questions
- *Why aren't liars believed even when they are telling the truth?*

- *How does it feel when somebody doesn't believe what you are saying?*

4

THURSDAY

Half the truth is often a lie.

—proverb

Reflection Question
- *What is an example of telling half the truth that is actually telling a lie?*

5

FRIDAY

He who permits himself to tell a lie once finds it much easier to do it a second and third time, till eventually it becomes a habit.

—Thomas Jefferson

Reflection Question
- *If you had a habit of telling lies, what are some things you could do to help yourself break this habit?*

Honesty

HONESTY

Character is what you do when nobody's looking.

—J.C. Watts

HONESTY

Honesty is the best policy.

—Miguel de Cervantes

"CHARACTER QUOTATIONS" Tom Lickona and Matt Davidson
Kagan Publishing • 1(800) 933-2667 • www.KaganOnline.com

HONESTY

Liars are not believed when they speak the truth.

—proverb

"CHARACTER QUOTATIONS" Tom Lickona and Matt Davidson
Kagan Publishing • 1(800) 933-2667 • www.KaganOnline.com

HONESTY

Half the truth is often a lie.

—proverb

HONESTY

He who permits himself to tell a lie once finds it much easier to do it a second and third time, till eventually it becomes a habit.

—Thomas Jefferson

❝CHARACTER QUOTATIONS❞ Tom Lickona and Matt Davidson
Kagan Publishing • 1(800) 933-2667 • www.KaganOnline.com

HONESTY

"CHARACTER QUOTATIONS" Tom Lickona and Matt Davidson
Kagan Publishing • 1(800) 933-2667 • www.KaganOnline.com

GRATITUDE

THE QUALITY OF BEING THANKFUL; SHOWING APPRECIATION.

WEEK 10

TUESDAY

Be happy with what you have, and you will have plenty to be happy about.
—Irish proverb

Reflection Question
• *How can we help ourselves remain grateful for the blessings we have?*

MONDAY

No duty is more urgent than that of returning thanks.
—St. Ambrose

Reflection Question
• *Why is this true?*

ACTION ASSIGNMENTS

• Create a list of things you are thankful for in your life (don't forget the things you can't see, like love). Share your list with a partner.

• As a class, create a composite list of the things you are thankful for.

• Each day thank someone for something you are grateful for, or write a thank-you note to someone expressing appreciation.

I complained that I had no shoes until I saw a man who had no feet.

—Daryl Germaine

Reflection Question

- *How does being aware of others' needs help us be more thankful for what we have?*

An attitude of gratitude creates blessings.

—Sir John Templeton

Reflection Question

- *Why does being grateful make us feel better?*

We never appreciate the value of water until the well runs dry.

—Ben Franklin

Reflection Questions

- *What are some things or people in your life that you take for granted?*

- *How could you show more appreciation for these things or people?*

Thank You

GRATITUDE

No duty is more urgent than that of returning thanks.

—St. Ambrose

Gratitude

Thank You

GRATITUDE

Be happy with what you have, and you will have plenty to be happy about.

—Irish proverb

Gratitude

"CHARACTER QUOTATIONS" Tom Lickona and Matt Davidson
Kagan Publishing • 1(800) 933-2667 • www.KaganOnline.com

Thank You

GRATITUDE

I complained that I had no shoes until I saw a man who had no feet.

—Daryl Germaine

Gratitude

"CHARACTER QUOTATIONS" Tom Lickona and Matt Davidson
Kagan Publishing • 1(800) 933-2667 • www.KaganOnline.com

Thank You

GRATITUDE

An attitude of gratitude creates blessings.

—Sir John Templeton

Gratitude

"CHARACTER QUOTATIONS" **Tom Lickona and Matt Davidson**
Kagan Publishing • 1(800) 933-2667 • www.KaganOnline.com

Thank You

GRATITUDE

We never appreciate the value of water until the well runs dry.

—Ben Franklin

"CHARACTER QUOTATIONS" Tom Lickona and Matt Davidson
Kagan Publishing • 1(800) 933-2667 • www.KaganOnline.com

GRATITUDE

Thank You

"CHARACTER QUOTATIONS" Tom Lickona and Matt Davidson
Kagan Publishing • 1(800) 933-2667 • www.KaganOnline.com

WORK

EFFORT DIRECTED TOWARD
PRODUCING OR ACCOMPLISHING
SOMETHING.

WEEK 11

TUESDAY

**Nothing worth having ever
comes except as the result of
hard work.**
                    —Booker T. Washington

Reflection Question
- *What is something you had to work
  hard at to achieve?*

MONDAY

**Perhaps the most valuable
result of education is the
ability to make yourself do
the thing you have to do
when it ought to be done,
whether you like it or not.**
                    —Thomas Huxley

Reflection Question
- *Why is it important to be able to make
  yourself do something you don't want
  to do?*

ACTION
ASSIGNMENTS

- Read about the life of Booker T.
  Washington (in an encyclopedia or
  biography). How did hard work help him
  to succeed?

- Interview an adult in your family or
  school. Ask, "Why is it important to work
  hard? How has working hard helped you
  in your life?"

- Choose something to work harder on
  this week; make a plan for how you will
  do that.

3
Genius is 1% inspiration and 99% perspiration.
—Thomas Edison

Reflection Questions
- *What does this mean? (Put it in your own words.)*

- *Why is this true?*

4
Laziness may appear attractive, but work gives satisfaction.
—Anne Frank (teenage girl, author of *Diary of Anne Frank*)

Reflection Question
- *Why does work lead to a feeling of satisfaction while laziness does not?*

5
One of the best prizes that life offers is the chance to work hard at work worth doing.
—Theodore Roosevelt

Reflection Question
- *What is a goal you are trying hard to achieve?*

WORK

Perhaps the most valuable result of education is the ability to make yourself do the thing you have to do when it ought to be done, whether you like it or not.

—Thomas Huxley

Work

WORK

Nothing worth having ever comes except as the result of hard work.

—Booker T. Washington

"CHARACTER QUOTATIONS" **Tom Lickona and Matt Davidson**
Kagan Publishing • 1(800) 933-2667 • www.KaganOnline.com

WORK

Genius is 1% inspiration and 99% perspiration.

—Thomas Edison

"CHARACTER QUOTATIONS" Tom Lickona and Matt Davidson
Kagan Publishing • 1(800) 933-2667 • www.KaganOnline.com

WORK

Laziness may appear attractive, but work gives satisfaction.

—Anne Frank
(teenage girl, author
of *Diary of Anne Frank*)

Work

"CHARACTER QUOTATIONS" Tom Lickona and Matt Davidson
Kagan Publishing • 1(800) 933-2667 • www.KaganOnline.com

WORK

One of the best prizes that life offers is the chance to work hard at work worth doing.

—Theodore Roosevelt

WORK

"CHARACTER QUOTATIONS" Tom Lickona and Matt Davidson
Kagan Publishing • 1(800) 933-2667 • www.KaganOnline.com

FRIENDSHIP

AN ATTACHMENT BASED ON FEELINGS OF AFFECTION AND ESTEEM.

WEEK 12

2

A friend in need is a friend indeed.

—proverb

Reflection Question
• *Why is it important for friends to stand by each other in times of need?*

MONDAY

1

If you want to have a friend, be a friend.
—Ralph Waldo Emerson

Reflection Question
• *What are some ways to be a good friend?*

ACTION ASSIGNMENTS

• Interview an adult in your family. Ask, "Who is a good friend to you? What qualities make that person a good friend? What qualities should I look for in a friend?"

• As a class, create a composite list of the qualities needed to be a good friend.

• This week, try to get to know two other people that you don't know very well. Do this by asking them questions about things they like to do, things they're good at, things about their family, etc.

WEDNESDAY

You can make more friends in two months by becoming really interested in other people than you can in two years by trying to get other people interested in you.

—Dale Carnegie

Reflection Question
• *Why is this good advice?*

THURSDAY

Whoever gossips to you will gossip about you.

—Spanish proverb

Reflection Questions
• *Do you think this is true? Explain.*

• *What can you do to help prevent spreading gossip about someone?*

FRIDAY

A false friend is worse than an open enemy.

—proverb

Reflection Questions
• *What is a "false friend"?*

• *Why is it important to be a good friend?*

FRIENDSHIP

If you want to have a friend, be a friend.

—Ralph Waldo Emerson

"CHARACTER QUOTATIONS" Tom Lickona and Matt Davidson
Kagan Publishing • 1(800) 933-2667 • www.KaganOnline.com

FRIENDSHIP

A friend in need is a friend indeed.

—proverb

"CHARACTER QUOTATIONS" Tom Lickona and Matt Davidson
Kagan Publishing • 1(800) 933-2667 • www.KaganOnline.com

FRIENDSHIP

You can make more friends in two months by becoming really interested in other people than you can in two years by trying to get other people interested in you.

—Dale Carnegie

Friendship

FRIENDSHIP

Whoever gossips to you will gossip about you.

—Spanish proverb

"CHARACTER QUOTATIONS" Tom Lickona and Matt Davidson
Kagan Publishing • 1(800) 933-2667 • www.KaganOnline.com

FRIENDSHIP

A false friend is worse than an open enemy.

—proverb

FRIENDSHIP

❝CHARACTER QUOTATIONS❞ Tom Lickona and Matt Davidson
Kagan Publishing • 1(800) 933-2667 • www.KaganOnline.com

FORGIVENESS

WEEK 13

GIVING UP CLAIM TO
COMPENSATION FOR AN
OFFENSE; CEASING TO FEEL
RESENTMENT AGAINST THE
OFFENDER.

TUESDAY

**He who asks for forgiveness
for his offenses must grant it
to others.**

—**Horace**

Reflection Question
- *How can you help yourself forgive someone you are upset with?*

MONDAY

Let bygones be bygones.
—**proverb**

Reflection Questions
- *Why is it important to get over a bad experience that you've had with a person?*

- *If you had an argument or bad experience with someone, what happens if you don't forgive that person?*

ACTION ASSIGNMENTS

- Write about, or discuss in pairs, a time when somebody forgave you for something wrong you did. Describe how it felt to be forgiven.

- As a class, discuss: "What feelings often make it hard for us to forgive another? What are some things we can do to overcome those feelings?"

- Decide as a class how to "let bygones be bygones."

- Get in the habit of apologizing right away whenever you do something wrong and even saying, "Please forgive me."

The best way to get the last word is to apologize.

—anonymous

Reflection Questions
- *What are the specific things that make for a good apology, one that really makes a person feel better?*

- *How does it make you feel when someone won't sincerely apologize for a wrong they've done?*

"I can forgive, but I cannot forget" is only another way of saying, "I cannot forgive."

—Henry Ward Beecher

Reflection Question
- *Why is it sometimes hard to forgive others?*

To err is human, to forgive is divine.

—Alexander Pope

Reflection Question
- *What is this quote telling us?*

"CHARACTER QUOTATIONS" Tom Lickona and Matt Davidson
Kagan Publishing • **1(800) 933-2667** • **www.KaganOnline.com**

115

FORGIVENESS

Let bygones be bygones.

—proverb

Forgiveness

FORGIVENESS

He who asks for forgiveness for his offenses must grant it to others.

—Horace

Forgiveness

"CHARACTER QUOTATIONS" Tom Lickona and Matt Davidson
Kagan Publishing • 1(800) 933-2667 • www.KaganOnline.com

FORGIVENESS

The best way to get the last word is to apologize.

—anonymous

"CHARACTER QUOTATIONS" Tom Lickona and Matt Davidson
Kagan Publishing • 1(800) 933-2667 • www.KaganOnline.com

FORGIVENESS

"I can forgive, but I cannot forget" is only another way of saying, "I cannot forgive."

—Henry Ward Beecher

"CHARACTER QUOTATIONS" Tom Lickona and Matt Davidson
Kagan Publishing • 1(800) 933-2667 • www.KaganOnline.com

FORGIVENESS

To err is human, to forgive is divine.

—Alexander Pope

"CHARACTER QUOTATIONS" Tom Lickona and Matt Davidson
Kagan Publishing • 1(800) 933-2667 • www.KaganOnline.com

FORGIVENESS

"CHARACTER QUOTATIONS" Tom Lickona and Matt Davidson
Kagan Publishing • 1(800) 933-2667 • www.KaganOnline.com

GENEROSITY

THE QUALITY OF GIVING MORE THAN IS REQUIRED.

WEEK 14

TUESDAY

2

Real generosity is doing something nice for someone who will never find out.
—Frank A. Clark

Reflection Question
• *Having somebody recognize you and thank you is one reason to do something kind; what are some other reasons?*

MONDAY

1

They who give have all things; they who withhold have nothing.
—Hindu proverb

Reflection Question
• *What does it mean to say that giving to others helps us to "have all things"?*

ACTION ASSIGNMENTS

• Put everybody's name in your class in a hat. The name you draw is your "secret pal" for that week.

• Then, as a class, generate a list of nice things you could do for your "secret pal." Each day do something nice for your secret pal without that person knowing it was you.

WEDNESDAY

It is better to give than to receive.

—Jesus

Reflection Question
• *Why is it better to give than receive?*

THURSDAY

The more we share, the more we have.

—Leonard Nimoy

Reflection Question
• *What does this mean?*

FRIDAY

Generosity is the bone shared with the dog when you are just as hungry as the dog.

—Jack London

Reflection Question
• *Which is more difficult: sharing when you have more than enough of something, or sharing when you barely have enough for yourself? Why?*

Generosity

"CHARACTER QUOTATIONS" Tom Lickona and Matt Davidson
Kagan Publishing • 1(800) 933-2667 • www.KaganOnline.com

GENEROSITY

They who give have all things; they who withhold have nothing.

—Hindu proverb

Generosity

"CHARACTER QUOTATIONS" Tom Lickona and Matt Davidson
Kagan Publishing • 1(800) 933-2667 • www.KaganOnline.com

GENEROSITY

Real generosity is doing something nice for someone who will never find out.

—Frank A. Clark

"CHARACTER QUOTATIONS" Tom Lickona and Matt Davidson
Kagan Publishing • 1(800) 933-2667 • www.KaganOnline.com

GENEROSITY

It is better to give than to receive.

—Jesus

Generosity

"CHARACTER QUOTATIONS" Tom Lickona and Matt Davidson
Kagan Publishing • 1(800) 933-2667 • www.KaganOnline.com

GENEROSITY

The more we share, the more we have.

—Leonard Nimoy

"CHARACTER QUOTATIONS" Tom Lickona and Matt Davidson
Kagan Publishing • 1(800) 933-2667 • www.KaganOnline.com

GENEROSITY

Generosity is the bone shared with the dog when you are just as hungry as the dog.

—Jack London

"CHARACTER QUOTATIONS" Tom Lickona and Matt Davidson
Kagan Publishing • 1(800) 933-2667 • www.KaganOnline.com

GENEROSITY

CHARACTER QUOTATIONS Tom Lickona and Matt Davidson
Kagan Publishing • 1(800) 933-2667 • www.KaganOnline.com

COOPERATION

WORKING TOGETHER FOR A
COMMON PURPOSE.

WEEK 15

TUESDAY

2

Three persons helping each other can do as much as six working alone.

—Spanish proverb

Reflection Question
- *How does working together help us to accomplish more than we could by working alone?*

MONDAY

1

It is one of the most beautiful compensations of life that no man can sincerely try to help another without helping himself.

—Ralph Waldo Emerson

Reflection Question
- *How do you help yourself when you help others?*

ACTION ASSIGNMENTS

- In small groups, generate as many responses as you can to the sentence, "A group works together best when..."

- As a class, make a composite list of your statements.

- This week, when you do an activity with a partner or small group, review the list before you begin. Together, choose one thing from the list you can improve on. At the end of the activity, evaluate how well you did. Make a plan to do even better next time.

WEDNESDAY

Many hands make light work.

—proverb

Reflection Question
• *What is one household chore you could do in order to lighten the work for somebody else?*

THURSDAY

None of us is as smart as all of us.

—classroom poster

Reflection Question
• *Why is this true?*

FRIDAY

A single twig breaks, but a bundle of twigs is strong.

—Tecumseh (Chief of Shawnee tribe who sought to form an alliance of all Native American nations)

Reflection Question
• *What does this quote tell us?*

COOPERATION

It is one of the most beautiful compensations of life that no man can sincerely try to help another without helping himself.

—Ralph Waldo Emerson

"CHARACTER QUOTATIONS" Tom Lickona and Matt Davidson
Kagan Publishing • 1(800) 933-2667 • www.KaganOnline.com

COOPERATION

Three persons helping each other can do as much as six working alone.

—Spanish proverb

COOPERATION

Many hands make light work.

—proverb

COOPERATION

None of us is as smart as all of us.

—classroom poster

"CHARACTER QUOTATIONS" Tom Lickona and Matt Davidson
Kagan Publishing • 1(800) 933-2667 • www.KaganOnline.com

COOPERATION

A single twig breaks, but a bundle of twigs is strong.

—Tecumseh
(Chief of Shawnee tribe who sought to form an alliance of all Native American nations)

Cooperation

"CHARACTER QUOTATIONS" Tom Lickona and Matt Davidson
Kagan Publishing • 1(800) 933-2667 • www.KaganOnline.com

COOPERATION

137

CONFIDENCE

BELIEF IN ONESELF;
SELF-ASSURANCE.

WEEK 16

TUESDAY

2

Whether you think you can or think you can't, you're right.

—Henry Ford

Reflection Question
- *How might negative thoughts keep us from accomplishing a goal?*

MONDAY

1

Conceive it, believe it, achieve it.

—maxim

Reflection Question
- *Why is it important to believe in yourself and your abilities if you want to attain a goal?*

ACTION ASSIGNMENTS

- A "personal power phrase" is a short statement or phrase that people use to help them create or maintain confidence. "Conceive it, believe it, achieve it," "Just do it," and "Whether you think you can or think you can't, you're right" are examples. Create or find a personal power phrase that you would like to use. (You may also wish to add graphics or drawings to personalize your power phrase.)

- For one week, write down the times when you use your personal power phrase and how it helped you.

Don't make yourself a mouse, or the cat will eat you.

—A.B. Cheales

Reflection Question
- *How does self-confidence prevent others from taking advantage of us?*

You gain strength, courage and confidence by every experience in which you must look fear in the face. You must do the thing you think you cannot do.

—Eleanor Roosevelt

Reflection Question
- *What is one thing you want to do that you're not very good at right now? How can you gain the confidence to do that?*

He who has lost his confidence can lose nothing more.

—Boiste

Reflection Question
- *Why is it important to have self-confidence?*

CONFIDENCE

Conceive it, believe it, achieve it.

—maxim

CONFIDENCE

Whether you think you can or think you can't, you're right.

—Henry Ford

"CHARACTER QUOTATIONS" Tom Lickona and Matt Davidson
Kagan Publishing • 1(800) 933-2667 • www.KaganOnline.com

CONFIDENCE

Don't make yourself a mouse, or the cat will eat you.

—A.B. Cheales

Confidence

"CHARACTER QUOTATIONS" Tom Lickona and Matt Davidson
Kagan Publishing • 1(800) 933-2667 • www.KaganOnline.com

CONFIDENCE

You gain strength, courage and confidence by every experience in which you must look fear in the face. You must do the thing you think you cannot do.

—Eleanor Roosevelt

Confidence

"CHARACTER QUOTATIONS" Tom Lickona and Matt Davidson
Kagan Publishing • 1(800) 933-2667 • www.KaganOnline.com

CONFIDENCE

He who has lost his confidence can lose nothing more.

—Boiste

"CHARACTER QUOTATIONS" Tom Lickona and Matt Davidson
Kagan Publishing • 1(800) 933-2667 • www.KaganOnline.com

CONFIDENCE

"CHARACTER QUOTATIONS" Tom Lickona and Matt Davidson
Kagan Publishing • 1(800) 933-2667 • www.KaganOnline.com

TOLERANCE/ DIVERSITY

RESPECT FOR OTHERS' FREEDOM OF CONSCIENCE; APPRECIATION OF DIFFERENCES.

WEEK 17

TUESDAY

2

Each of us is different. Expect it. Respect it. Accept it.

—school poster

Reflection Questions
- *What are some ways that students sometimes don't respect and accept those who are different from themselves?*

- *What is one thing you can do when you see someone being teased, bullied, or left out because that person is "different"?*

MONDAY

1

I dream that my children will one day live in a nation where they will be judged not by the color of their skin but by the content of their character.

—Martin Luther King, Jr.

Reflection Question
- *What does the phrase "content of character" mean?*

ACTION ASSIGNMENTS

- Partner with someone you don't already know well. Together make a list of ways you are alike and ways you are different. Answer questions such as, "What is your favorite food? What are two things you like to do? What is something you're good at? What's your favorite subject or activity in school?"

- As a class, form a circle. Partners then introduce each other to the whole group. The first person says, "My partner was ___. A way we're *alike* is ____." Then the second person says, "My partner was ___. A way that we're *different* is ____."

- As a class, discuss what was valuable about learning about similarities and differences.

3

I don't like that man. I'll have to get to know him better.

—Abraham Lincoln

Reflection Questions
• *Why do you think Lincoln said this?*

• *When is a time you got to like someone after you got to know that person better?*

4

I will not judge people because of where they live, the color of their skin, their abilities, or their spiritual beliefs. I can and will find the good in all people.

—Children's Diversity Pledge

Reflection Question
• *How can you try to "find the good" in other people?*

5

Grant that I may not criticize my neighbor until I have walked a mile in his moccasins.

—Native American saying

Reflection Question
• *What does this mean? (Put it in your own words.)*

TOLERANCE/ DIVERSITY

I dream that my children will one day live in a nation where they will be judged not by the color of their skin but by the content of their character.

—Martin Luther King, Jr.

CHARACTER QUOTATIONS Tom Lickona and Matt Davidson
Kagan Publishing • 1(800) 933-2667 • www.KaganOnline.com

TOLERANCE/ DIVERSITY

Each of us is different. Expect it. Respect it. Accept it.

—school poster

Tolerance / Diversity

"CHARACTER QUOTATIONS" Tom Lickona and Matt Davidson
Kagan Publishing • 1(800) 933-2667 • www.KaganOnline.com

TOLERANCE/ DIVERSITY

I don't like that man. I'll have to get to know him better.

—Abraham Lincoln

Tolerance / Diversity

"CHARACTER QUOTATIONS" Tom Lickona and Matt Davidson
Kagan Publishing • 1(800) 933-2667 • www.KaganOnline.com

TOLERANCE/ DIVERSITY

I will not judge people because of where they live, the color of their skin, their abilities, or their spiritual beliefs. I can and will find the good in all people.

—Children's Diversity Pledge

"CHARACTER QUOTATIONS" Tom Lickona and Matt Davidson
Kagan Publishing • 1(800) 933-2667 • www.KaganOnline.com

TOLERANCE/ DIVERSITY

Grant that I may not criticize my neighbor until I have walked a mile in his moccasins.

—Native American saying

"CHARACTER QUOTATIONS" Tom Lickona and Matt Davidson
Kagan Publishing • 1(800) 933-2667 • www.KaganOnline.com

TOLERANCE/ DIVERSITY

JUSTICE/ FAIRNESS

TREATING PEOPLE AS THEY DESERVE TO BE TREATED; RESPECTING THE RIGHTS OF ALL.

WEEK 18

TUESDAY

2

Do unto others as you would have them do unto you.
—The Golden Rule

Reflection Question
- *What does this mean? (Put it in your own words.)*

MONDAY

1

Life isn't fair, but you and I should be.
—anonymous

Reflection Question
- *Why is it important to be fair?*

ACTION ASSIGNMENTS

- This week, at the beginning of each day, think about how you will try to follow the Golden Rule ("treat others as you wish to be treated"). At the end of the school day, write down one way you followed the Golden Rule and one way you didn't.

- As a class, brainstorm a list of positive things you can do if you see or hear someone being mean to another person.

- When you see or hear somebody being mean to another person, do something to try to stop it or to show your disapproval.

3

Two wrongs don't make a right.

—maxim

Reflection Question

• *What does this saying tell you to do if somebody calls you a name?*

4

Never dare to judge until you have heard the other side.

—Euripides

Reflection Question

• *Why is it always important to hear the other side of a story before making a judgment?*

5

There are two kinds of injustice: harming another, and failing to protect another from injury when we can.

—Cicero

Reflection Questions

• *What kind of behaviors do you see in school that hurt other people?*

• *What is one thing you could do to try to stop those behaviors?*

JUSTICE/ FAIRNESS

Life isn't fair, but you and I should be.

—anonymous

JUSTICE/ FAIRNESS

Do unto others as you would have them do unto you.

—The Golden Rule

"CHARACTER QUOTATIONS" Tom Lickona and Matt Davidson
Kagan Publishing • 1(800) 933-2667 • www.KaganOnline.com

JUSTICE/
FAIRNESS

Two wrongs don't make a right.

—maxim

❝CHARACTER QUOTATIONS❞ Tom Lickona and Matt Davidson
Kagan Publishing • 1(800) 933-2667 • www.KaganOnline.com

JUSTICE/ FAIRNESS

Never dare to judge until you have heard the other side.

—Euripides

"CHARACTER QUOTATIONS" Tom Lickona and Matt Davidson
Kagan Publishing • 1(800) 933-2667 • www.KaganOnline.com

JUSTICE/ FAIRNESS

There are two kinds of injustice: harming another, and failing to protect another from injury when we can.

—Cicero

JUSTICE/ FAIRNESS

SELF-CONTROL/ SELF-DISCIPLINE

RESTRAINING ONE'S FEELINGS AND ACTIONS.

WEEK 19

TUESDAY

2

Discipline yourself, and others won't have to.
—John Wooden
(UCLA men's basketball coach, whose teams won a record ten national championships)

Reflection Question
• *What does this mean?*

MONDAY

1

There is only one corner of the universe you can be certain of improving, and that is your own self.
—Aldous Huxley

Reflection Question
• *What is one thing you are willing to do to try to become a better person?*

ACTION ASSIGNMENTS

• Create a personal strategy for controlling your emotions (e.g., count to 10—or higher).

• In small groups, share your strategies.

• As a class, create a composite list of self-control strategies. Choose one and begin to use it. At the end of the week, as a group, share how you did.

3

Be patient in one moment of anger, and you will escape a hundred days of sorrow.

—Chinese proverb

Reflection Question
- *Why does giving in to anger often lead to regrets?*

4

When angry, count to 10 before you speak. If you are very angry, count to 100.

—Thomas Jefferson

Reflection Questions
- *Have you ever tried this?*

- *How does counting help us to control anger?*

5

The less you control what you do, the more what you do controls you.

—Don Stanton

Reflection Question
- *What does this mean?*

Self-Discipline / Self-Control

SELF-CONTROL/ SELF-DISCIPLINE

There is only one corner of the universe you can be certain of improving, and that is your own self.

—Aldous Huxley

SELF-CONTROL/ SELF-DISCIPLINE

Discipline yourself, and others won't have to.

—John Wooden
(UCLA men's basketball coach, whose teams won a record ten national championships)

Self-Control / Self-Discipline

SELF-CONTROL/ SELF-DISCIPLINE

Be patient in one moment of anger, and you will escape a hundred days of sorrow.

—Chinese proverb

"CHARACTER QUOTATIONS" Tom Lickona and Matt Davidson
Kagan Publishing • 1(800) 933-2667 • www.KaganOnline.com

SELF-CONTROL/ SELF-DISCIPLINE

When angry, count to 10 before you speak. If you are very angry, count to 100.

—Thomas Jefferson

"CHARACTER QUOTATIONS" Tom Lickona and Matt Davidson
Kagan Publishing • 1(800) 933-2667 • www.KaganOnline.com

SELF-CONTROL/ SELF-DISCIPLINE

The less you control what you do, the more what you do controls you.

—Don Stanton

"CHARACTER QUOTATIONS" Tom Lickona and Matt Davidson
Kagan Publishing • 1(800) 933-2667 • www.KaganOnline.com

SELF-CONTROL/ SELF-DISCIPLINE

"CHARACTER QUOTATIONS" **Tom Lickona and Matt Davidson**
Kagan Publishing • 1(800) 933-2667 • www.KaganOnline.com

FORTITUDE

THE INNER TOUGHNESS THAT
ENABLES US TO BE OUR BEST
IN THE FACE OF DIFFICULTIES.

WEEK 20

TUESDAY

2

There's no gain without pain.
—Ben Franklin

Reflection Question
• *What is something you have tried that took a lot of work to get better at?*

MONDAY

1

When the going gets tough, the tough get going.
—maxim

Reflection Question
• *What does this quote tell us about what we should do when we face difficulties in life?*

ACTION ASSIGNMENTS

• **Make a list of things that are particularly difficult or challenging for you.**

• **Choose one and make a plan for meeting that challenge.**

• **Share your plan with a partner. Get additional suggestions from your partner that might help your plan succeed.**

WEDNESDAY 3

A problem is a chance for you to do your best.
—Duke Ellington

Reflection Question
- *How can you help yourself do your best when you are facing a problem?*

THURSDAY 4

When everything seems to be going against you, remember that the airplane takes off against the wind.
—Henry Ford

Reflection Question
- *Why is it important to stick with things that are hard?*

FRIDAY 5

A smooth sea never made a skillful mariner.
—proverb

Reflection Question
- *Why is it better to try difficult things than to only do things that come easy for us?*

"CHARACTER QUOTATIONS" Tom Lickona and Matt Davidson
Kagan Publishing • 1(800) 933-2667 • www.KaganOnline.com

Fortitude

FORTITUDE

When the going gets tough, the tough get going.

—maxim

"CHARACTER QUOTATIONS" Tom Lickona and Matt Davidson
Kagan Publishing • 1(800) 933-2667 • www.KaganOnline.com

FORTITUDE

There's no gain without pain.

—Ben Franklin

FORTITUDE

A problem is a chance for you to do your best.

—Duke Ellington

"CHARACTER QUOTATIONS" Tom Lickona and Matt Davidson
Kagan Publishing • 1(800) 933-2667 • www.KaganOnline.com

FORTITUDE

When everything seems to be going against you, remember that the airplane takes off against the wind.

—Henry Ford

❝CHARACTER QUOTATIONS❞ Tom Lickona and Matt Davidson
Kagan Publishing • 1(800) 933-2667 • www.KaganOnline.com

FORTITUDE

A smooth sea never made a skillful mariner.

—proverb

FORTITUDE

"CHARACTER QUOTATIONS" Tom Lickona and Matt Davidson
Kagan Publishing • 1(800) 933-2667 • www.KaganOnline.com

COURAGE

THE QUALITY THAT ENABLES A PERSON TO MEET DIFFICULTY OR DANGER WITH FIRMNESS.

WEEK 21

TUESDAY

2

Never let the fear of striking out get in your way.

—Babe Ruth (held records for both home runs *and* strikeouts)

Reflection Question
• *What makes us afraid of trying new things?*

MONDAY

1

It is curious that physical courage should be so common and moral courage so rare.

—Mark Twain

Reflection Questions
• *How are physical courage and moral courage different?*

• *Why is moral courage less common than physical courage?*

ACTION ASSIGNMENTS

• As a class, read a book about a person who showed courage (e.g., *John Blair and the Great Hinckley Fire* by Josephine Nobisso). What did the main character in the story do that showed courage? Then, individually, write a paragraph about a time when you showed courage. Share it with a partner.

• During the next week, look for at least one example of courage in the news, at home, or in your school. As a class, make a bulletin board of all the different examples. Discuss these: How are the examples similar or different? In each case, how do you think the person overcame fear?

• As an individual, look for opportunities to show courage in your school, home, or community.

WEDNESDAY

Courage is mastery of fear, not absence of fear.

—Mark Twain

Reflection Questions

• *What is something that you used to be afraid of, but are not afraid of anymore?*

• *How did you get over your fear?*

THURSDAY

He who is afraid of a thing gives it power over him.

—Moorish proverb

Reflection Questions

• *How does something we are afraid of have power over us?*

• *What are some things you can do to overcome something you are afraid of?*

FRIDAY

To see what is right and not to do it is cowardice.

—Confucius

Reflection Questions

• *If we see someone being teased or bullied in school, what could we do to stop it?*

• *What are some things that might keep us from taking action?*

Courage

"CHARACTER QUOTATIONS" Tom Lickona and Matt Davidson
Kagan Publishing • 1(800) 933-2667 • www.KaganOnline.com

COURAGE

It is curious that physical courage should be so common and moral courage so rare.

—Mark Twain

COURAGE

Never let the fear of striking out get in your way.

—Babe Ruth
(held records for both
home runs *and* strikeouts)

"CHARACTER QUOTATIONS" Tom Lickona and Matt Davidson
Kagan Publishing • 1(800) 933-2667 • www.KaganOnline.com

COURAGE

Courage is mastery of fear, not absence of fear.

—Mark Twain

"CHARACTER QUOTATIONS" Tom Lickona and Matt Davidson
Kagan Publishing • 1(800) 933-2667 • www.KaganOnline.com

COURAGE

He who is afraid of a thing gives it power over him.

—Moorish proverb

"CHARACTER QUOTATIONS" Tom Lickona and Matt Davidson
Kagan Publishing • 1(800) 933-2667 • www.KaganOnline.com

COURAGE

To see what is right and not to do it is cowardice.

—Confucius

"CHARACTER QUOTATIONS" Tom Lickona and Matt Davidson
Kagan Publishing • 1(800) 933-2667 • www.KaganOnline.com

COURAGE

"CHARACTER QUOTATIONS" Tom Lickona and Matt Davidson
Kagan Publishing • 1(800) 933-2667 • www.KaganOnline.com

CITIZENSHIP

THE WAYS WE CONTRIBUTE TO
OUR COMMUNITY AND COUNTRY.

WEEK 22

TUESDAY

2

Do all the good you can, in all the ways you can, to all the people you can.

—John Wesley

Reflection Question
• *What is some good you can do today?*

MONDAY

1

Within the character of the citizen lies the welfare of the nation.

—Cicero

Reflection Question
• *How does the character of citizens affect the welfare of the nation?*

ACTION ASSIGNMENTS

• As a class, identify some needs in your school or community. Choose one and develop and carry out a plan for how your class can help to meet that need.

• Write essays individually or design posters in small groups on these questions: What does it mean to be a good citizen of one's country? What does it mean to be a good citizen of the world?

3

The only thing necessary for the triumph of evil is for good people to do nothing.
—Edmund Burke

Reflection Questions
- *Why is this true?*

- *What is an example of this?*

4

Life's most persistent question is, "What are you doing for others?"
—Martin Luther King, Jr.

Reflection Question
- *How would you answer this question?*

5

The life of the nation is secure only while the nation is honest, truthful, and virtuous.
—Frederick Douglas

Reflection Question
- *Why is the life of the country in danger when people are not honest and good?*

"CHARACTER QUOTATIONS" Tom Lickona and Matt Davidson
Kagan Publishing • 1(800) 933-2667 • www.KaganOnline.com

CITIZENSHIP

Within the character of the citizen lies the welfare of the nation.

—Cicero

"CHARACTER QUOTATIONS" Tom Lickona and Matt Davidson
Kagan Publishing • 1(800) 933-2667 • www.KaganOnline.com

CITIZENSHIP

Do all the good you can, in all the ways you can, to all the people you can.

—John Wesley

"CHARACTER QUOTATIONS" Tom Lickona and Matt Davidson
Kagan Publishing • 1(800) 933-2667 • www.KaganOnline.com

CITIZENSHIP

The only thing necessary for the triumph of evil is for good people to do nothing.

—Edmund Burke

"CHARACTER QUOTATIONS" Tom Lickona and Matt Davidson
Kagan Publishing • 1(800) 933-2667 • www.KaganOnline.com

CITIZENSHIP

**Life's most persistent
question is, "What are you
doing for others?"**

—Martin Luther King, Jr.

CHARACTER QUOTATIONS Tom Lickona and Matt Davidson
Kagan Publishing • 1(800) 933-2667 • www.KaganOnline.com

CITIZENSHIP

The life of the nation is secure only while the nation is honest, truthful, and virtuous.

—Frederick Douglas

"CHARACTER QUOTATIONS" Tom Lickona and Matt Davidson
Kagan Publishing • 1(800) 933-2667 • www.KaganOnline.com

CITIZENSHIP

“CHARACTER QUOTATIONS” Tom Lickona and Matt Davidson
Kagan Publishing • 1(800) 933-2667 • www.KaganOnline.com

EFFORT

THE DELIBERATE EXERTION OF MENTAL OR PHYSICAL POWER.

WEEK 23

TUESDAY

If you can't excel with talent, triumph with effort.

—Dave Weinbaum

Reflection Question
• *What is something you achieved not because you were naturally good at it, but because you worked really hard?*

MONDAY

Make the most of yourself, for that is all there is of you.

—Ralph Waldo Emerson

Reflection Question
• *What does it mean to "make the most of yourself"?*

ACTION ASSIGNMENTS

• As a class, discuss how you know when you've given your best effort.

• Choose one school subject where making a better effort would help you to improve. Make a plan for how you will try harder in this subject this week. With your teacher and/or an adult in your family, share your plan and get additional suggestions.

3

It's not enough to stare up the steps; you have to step up the stairs.
—Coach Hugh Moyer

Reflection Question
- *How can you help yourself take the first difficult step to learn or do something?*

4

The impossible takes just a little longer to accomplish.
—Wilma Rudolph

Reflection Question
- *What is something that seemed impossible to you, but you eventually did it because you didn't give up?*

5

There are no shortcuts to anyplace worth going.
—anonymous

Reflection Question
- *What does this mean?*

CHARACTER QUOTATIONS Tom Lickona and Matt Davidson
Kagan Publishing • 1(800) 933-2667 • www.KaganOnline.com

EFFORT

**Make the most of yourself,
for that is all there is of you.**

—Ralph Waldo Emerson

"CHARACTER QUOTATIONS" Tom Lickona and Matt Davidson
Kagan Publishing • 1(800) 933-2667 • www.KaganOnline.com

EFFORT

If you can't excel with talent, triumph with effort.

—Dave Weinbaum

"CHARACTER QUOTATIONS" Tom Lickona and Matt Davidson
Kagan Publishing • 1(800) 933-2667 • www.KaganOnline.com

EFFORT

It's not enough to stare up the steps; you have to step up the stairs.

—Coach Hugh Moyer

Effort

"CHARACTER QUOTATIONS" Tom Lickona and Matt Davidson
Kagan Publishing • 1(800) 933-2667 • www.KaganOnline.com

EFFORT

The impossible takes just a little longer to accomplish.

—Wilma Rudolph

"CHARACTER QUOTATIONS" Tom Lickona and Matt Davidson
Kagan Publishing • 1(800) 933-2667 • www.KaganOnline.com

EFFORT

There are no shortcuts to anyplace worth going.

—anonymous

"CHARACTER QUOTATIONS" Tom Lickona and Matt Davidson
Kagan Publishing • 1(800) 933-2667 • www.KaganOnline.com

EFFORT

"CHARACTER QUOTATIONS" Tom Lickona and Matt Davidson
Kagan Publishing • 1(800) 933-2667 • www.KaganOnline.com

CONSCIENCE

THE SENSE OF WHAT IS RIGHT OR WRONG IN ONE'S CONDUCT OR MOTIVES.

WEEK 24

MONDAY

1

Right is right, even if everyone is against it, and wrong is wrong, even if everyone is for it.

—William Penn

Reflection Question
• *What can you do if you find yourself in a situation where you disagree with what everybody is doing?*

TUESDAY

2

A conscience is the part of your mind that has the job of decision-maker. Most of the time I listen to it, but there are times when my conscience sleeps through an incident.

—fifth-grade student

Reflection Questions
• *When was a time that your conscience told you that you should (or should not) do something?*

• *How can you keep your conscience from "going to sleep"?*

ACTION ASSIGNMENTS

• Interview an adult or discuss as a class: "What is conscience? Why is it important to follow your conscience? When was a time that your conscience told you that you should (or should not) do something?"

• In small groups, share the results of your "conscience interviews." What did the person interviewed say in response to your questions, and what was the most important thing you each learned from the interview?

• This week, at the end of each day, examine your conscience. By writing in a journal or discussing with a partner, consider: How did I show good character today? How did I not show good character today? How will I show good character tomorrow?

Do not cut your conscience to fit this year's fashions.
—Catherine Cookson

Reflection Question
- *When is it a bad idea to go along with whatever the group is doing?*

THURSDAY

There is no pillow so soft as a clear conscience.
—French proverb

Reflection Question
- *When we do something wrong, why do we feel bad?*

FRIDAY

Let your conscience be your guide.
—Jiminy Cricket (character in the book *Pinocchio*)

Reflection Question
- *If your conscience tells you that you should (or should not) do something, what can you do to help yourself follow your conscience?*

"CHARACTER QUOTATIONS" Tom Lickona and Matt Davidson
Kagan Publishing • 1(800) 933-2667 • www.KaganOnline.com

CONSCIENCE

Right is right, even if everyone is against it, and wrong is wrong, even if everyone is for it.

—William Penn

"CHARACTER QUOTATIONS" Tom Lickona and Matt Davidson
Kagan Publishing • 1(800) 933-2667 • www.KaganOnline.com

CONSCIENCE

A conscience is the part of your mind that has the job of decision-maker. Most of the time I listen to it, but there are times when my conscience sleeps through an incident.

—Fifth-grade student

"CHARACTER QUOTATIONS" Tom Lickona and Matt Davidson
Kagan Publishing • 1(800) 933-2667 • www.KaganOnline.com

CONSCIENCE

Do not cut your conscience to fit this year's fashions.

—Catherine Cookson

Conscience

"CHARACTER QUOTATIONS" Tom Lickona and Matt Davidson
Kagan Publishing • 1(800) 933-2667 • www.KaganOnline.com

CONSCIENCE

There is no pillow so soft as a clear conscience.

—French proverb

Conscience

"CHARACTER QUOTATIONS" Tom Lickona and Matt Davidson
Kagan Publishing • 1(800) 933-2667 • www.KaganOnline.com

CONSCIENCE

Let your conscience be your guide.

**—Jiminy Cricket
(character in the book *Pinocchio*)**

Conscience

CONSCIENCE

RESPECT

WEEK 25

SHOWING REGARD FOR THE WORTH OF SOMEONE OR SOMETHING.

TUESDAY

2

I hope that all children today will grow up without hate and learn to respect one another, no matter what color they are.

—Rosa Parks

Reflection Question
• *Why do people sometimes dislike or even hate persons who are different from them?*

MONDAY

1

We cannot live better than by seeking to become better.

—Seneca

Reflection Question
• *What is one thing you can do this week to try to become a better person?*

ACTION ASSIGNMENTS

• In small groups, list answers to the following questions: (1) What are ways to show respect for parents/guardians? (2) What are ways to show respect for teachers? (3) What are ways to show respect for peers?

• Post the lists from each group. Individually, choose one item from each list and put it into practice.

Respect yourself if you want others to respect you.
—Baltassi Gracian

Reflection Questions

• *What does it mean to "respect yourself"?*

• *Why is it important to respect yourself if you want others to respect you?*

Treat all persons alike. Give them all an equal chance to live and grow. All were made by the same Great Spirit.
—Chief Joseph

Reflection Question

• *Why should we treat all persons equally?*

Honor your father and mother.
—The Fourth Commandment

Reflection Question

• *Why is it important to respect your parents/guardians?*

"CHARACTER QUOTATIONS" Tom Lickona and Matt Davidson
Kagan Publishing • 1(800) 933-2667 • www.KaganOnline.com

RESPECT

We cannot live better than by seeking to become better.

—Seneca

"CHARACTER QUOTATIONS" Tom Lickona and Matt Davidson
Kagan Publishing • 1(800) 933-2667 • www.KaganOnline.com

RESPECT

I hope that all children today will grow up without hate and learn to respect one another, no matter what color they are.

—Rosa Parks

"CHARACTER QUOTATIONS" Tom Lickona and Matt Davidson
Kagan Publishing • 1(800) 933-2667 • www.KaganOnline.com

RESPECT

Respect yourself if you want others to respect you.

—Baltassi Gracian

25.3 QUOTE OF THE DAY

RESPECT

Treat all persons alike. Give them all an equal chance to live and grow. All were made by the same Great Spirit.

—Chief Joseph

"CHARACTER QUOTATIONS" Tom Lickona and Matt Davidson
Kagan Publishing • 1(800) 933-2667 • www.KaganOnline.com

RESPECT

Honor your father and mother.

—The Fourth Commandment

"CHARACTER QUOTATIONS" Tom Lickona and Matt Davidson
Kagan Publishing • 1(800) 933-2667 • www.KaganOnline.com

RESPECT

"CHARACTER QUOTATIONS" Tom Lickona and Matt Davidson
Kagan Publishing • 1(800) 933-2667 • www.KaganOnline.com

PERSEVERANCE

THE QUALITY OF PERSISTING IN ANY UNDERTAKING, DESPITE DIFFICULTIES.

WEEK 26

TUESDAY

Failure is not falling down, but staying down.

—Mary Pickford

Reflection Question
- *What is something you can do, after you fail, to help yourself "get up" and keep trying?*

MONDAY

If you wish to succeed in life, make perseverance your close friend.

—James Addison

Reflection Question
- *How will perseverance help you succeed in life?*

ACTION ASSIGNMENTS

- Individually, look for positive examples in books, newspapers, magazines, etc., of people who have persevered and finally achieved their goals.

- As a class, share your examples. Then create a "Perseverance Bulletin Board" using the various examples.

WEDNESDAY 3

Persistence melts resistance.
—Spencer Kagan

Reflection Questions
- *Why is it a good idea to persist in the face of resistance?*

- *When might it not be a good idea?*

THURSDAY 4

Most of the things worth doing in the world were declared impossible before they were done.
—Thomas Edison

Reflection Question
- *What is an example of something that people thought was impossible before it was done?*

FRIDAY 5

Never, never, never give up!
—Winston Churchill

Reflection Question
- *How can a never-give-up attitude help you?*

PERSEVERANCE

If you wish to succeed in life, make perseverance your close friend.

—James Addison

PERSEVERANCE

Failure is not falling down, but staying down.

—Mary Pickford

"CHARACTER QUOTATIONS" **Tom Lickona and Matt Davidson**
Kagan Publishing • 1(800) 933-2667 • www.KaganOnline.com

PERSEVERANCE

Persistence melts resistance.

—Spencer Kagan

PERSEVERANCE

Most of the things worth doing in the world were declared impossible before they were done.

—Thomas Edison

PERSEVERANCE

Never, never, never give up!

—Winston Churchill

"CHARACTER QUOTATIONS" Tom Lickona and Matt Davidson
Kagan Publishing • 1(800) 933-2667 • www.KaganOnline.com

PERSEVERANCE

"CHARACTER QUOTATIONS" Tom Lickona and Matt Davidson
Kagan Publishing • 1(800) 933-2667 • www.KaganOnline.com

CHEERFULNESS

THE QUALITY OF EXPRESSING
OR PROMOTING GOOD SPIRITS.

WEEK 27

TUESDAY

2

The best way to cheer yourself up is to try to cheer somebody else up.

—Mark Twain

Reflection Question
- *If someone is feeling sad, what are some things you could do to cheer up him or her?*

MONDAY

1

Your smile is the most important thing you wear.

—anonymous

Reflection Question
- *Why is your smile important?*

ACTION ASSIGNMENTS

- This week, do the following experiment: Smile at everyone you see. Notice people's responses. Also notice how smiling at others makes you feel.

- As a class, discuss the results of this experiment and the power of being cheerful.

We may never know all the good a single smile can do.
—Mother Teresa

Reflection Questions
• *Why do smiles make us feel so good?*

• *How do they affect the people around us?*

We either drag others down or lift them up.
—Booker T. Washington

Reflection Question
• *How does not being cheerful bring others around us down?*

Those who bring sunshine to the lives of others cannot keep it from themselves.
—James Barrie

Reflection Question
• *What are two things you can do to make those around you feel better?*

CHEERFULNESS

Your smile is the most important thing you wear.

—anonymous

Cheerfulness

"CHARACTER QUOTATIONS" Tom Lickona and Matt Davidson
Kagan Publishing • 1(800) 933-2667 • www.KaganOnline.com

CHEERFULNESS

The best way to cheer yourself up is to try to cheer somebody else up.

—Mark Twain

CHEERFULNESS

We may never know all the good a single smile can do.

—Mother Teresa

Cheerfulness

CHEERFULNESS

We either drag others down or lift them up.

—Booker T. Washington

"CHARACTER QUOTATIONS" Tom Lickona and Matt Davidson
Kagan Publishing • 1(800) 933-2667 • www.KaganOnline.com

CHEERFULNESS

Those who bring sunshine to the lives of others cannot keep it from themselves.

—James Barrie

CHEERFULNESS

"CHARACTER QUOTATIONS" Tom Lickona and Matt Davidson
Kagan Publishing • 1(800) 933-2667 • www.KaganOnline.com

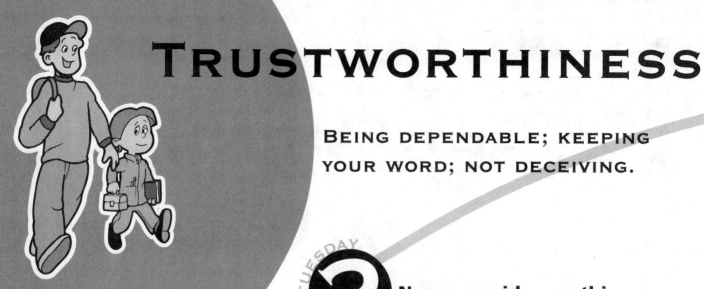

TRUSTWORTHINESS

BEING DEPENDABLE; KEEPING
YOUR WORD; NOT DECEIVING.

WEEK 28

TUESDAY

2

Never consider anything an advantage that will make you break your word.

—Marcus Aurelius Antonius

Reflection Question
• *Why is it important to keep your word?*

MONDAY

1

Actions speak louder than words.

—proverb

Reflection Question
• *Why is this true?*

ACTION ASSIGNMENTS

• Interview an adult family member. Ask, "Who is somebody you really trust? What are the specific things that person does to show that he or she is, in fact, worthy of your trust?"

• Make a list of things at home that you've promised to do (doing chores, keeping curfew, taking care of a sibling, etc.) that you sometimes fail to do in a dependable way. Choose one and make a plan for carrying out that commitment more dependably in the future.

Trust is what makes one person believe in another.

—Henry Mencker

Reflection Question
• *What does it mean to say that we "trust" somebody?*

Whoever can be trusted with small things can be trusted with large things.

—Jesus

Reflection Question
• *Why do people trust us more if we carry out our responsibilities?*

Few things help individuals more than to place responsibility on them, and to let them know that you trust them.

—Booker T. Washington

Reflection Question
• *What are some things we can do to earn the trust of another person?*

"CHARACTER QUOTATIONS" Tom Lickona and Matt Davidson
Kagan Publishing • 1(800) 933-2667 • www.KaganOnline.com

TRUSTWORTHINESS

Actions speak louder than words.

—proverb

"CHARACTER QUOTATIONS" Tom Lickona and Matt Davidson
Kagan Publishing • 1(800) 933-2667 • www.KaganOnline.com

TRUSTWORTHINESS

Never consider anything an advantage that will make you break your word.

—Marcus Aurelius Antonius

Trustworthiness

TRUSTWORTHINESS

Trust is what makes one person believe in another.

—Henry Mencker

Trustworthiness

"CHARACTER QUOTATIONS" Tom Lickona and Matt Davidson
Kagan Publishing • 1(800) 933-2667 • www.KaganOnline.com

TRUSTWORTHINESS

Whoever can be trusted with small things can be trusted with large things.

—Jesus

Trustworthiness

"CHARACTER QUOTATIONS" Tom Lickona and Matt Davidson
Kagan Publishing • 1(800) 933-2667 • www.KaganOnline.com

TRUSTWORTHINESS

Few things help individuals more than to place responsibility on them, and to let them know that you trust them.

—Booker T. Washington

Trustworthiness

TRUSTWORTHINESS

REPUTATION

HOW A PERSON IS KNOWN OR REMEMBERED BY OTHERS.

WEEK 29

TUESDAY

People are judged by the company they keep.

—proverb

Reflection Question
- *Why is important to surround yourself with good friends?*

MONDAY

It is nice to be important, but it is more important to be nice.

—proverb

Reflection Question
- *Why is it important to be nice?*

ACTION ASSIGNMENTS

- Imagine that a classmate is describing you to somebody who doesn't already know you. Write down three positive character qualities you would want that classmate to use to describe you.

- Share with a partner the three character qualities you named and how you try to show those qualities by what you say and do.

- Choose one of these three qualities that you might show more consistently. Make a plan for how you will do that and begin to put that into practice today.

242

3

It takes 20 years to build a reputation and 20 minutes to ruin it.

—Warren Buffett

Reflection Questions
- *What are some ways you can build a good reputation?*

- *What are some ways you can keep from hurting your reputation?*

4

A good name is better than riches.

—proverb

Reflection Question
- *How might a good name be better than riches?*

5

If someone says something unkind about you, live your life so that no one will believe it.

—anonymous

Reflection Question
- *What does this quote tell you about how to earn a good reputation?*

REPUTATION

It is nice to be important, but it is more important to be nice.

—proverb

"CHARACTER QUOTATIONS" Tom Lickona and Matt Davidson
Kagan Publishing • 1(800) 933-2667 • www.KaganOnline.com

REPUTATION

People are judged by the company they keep.

—proverb

Reputation

"CHARACTER QUOTATIONS" **Tom Lickona and Matt Davidson**
Kagan Publishing • 1(800) 933-2667 • www.KaganOnline.com

REPUTATION

It takes 20 years to build a reputation and 20 minutes to ruin it.

—Warren Buffett

CHARACTER QUOTATIONS Tom Lickona and Matt Davidson
Kagan Publishing • 1(800) 933-2667 • www.KaganOnline.com

REPUTATION

A good name is better than riches.

—proverb

REPUTATION

If someone says something unkind about you, live your life so that no one will believe it.

—anonymous

Reputation

REPUTATION

WORK

WEEK 30

EFFORT DIRECTED TOWARD
PRODUCING OR ACCOMPLISHING
SOMETHING.

TUESDAY

2

The harder you work, the luckier you get.

—Gary Player

Reflection Question
- *What does this mean?*

MONDAY

1

Without ambition, one starts nothing. Without work, one finishes nothing.

—Ralph Waldo Emerson

Reflection Question
- *What is an ambition you have—and how are you working on it?*

ACTION ASSIGNMENTS

- Make a list of after-school responsibilities you need to accomplish this week (e.g., chores, homework, studying for test, practice, etc.).

- Keep track of how you spend your time after school each day this week. At the end of each day, add up how you spent your time.

- At the end of each day, ask yourself, "Did I carry out all of my responsibilities as I well as I could have? How could I use my time more effectively tomorrow to fulfill all my responsibilities?"

- At the end of the week, discuss as a class what you learned about how you spend your time—and how you can spend it better in the future.

WEDNESDAY

Never put off until tomorrow what you can do today.

—Ben Franklin

Reflection Question
- *Why is it not a good idea to put off until tomorrow what you can do today?*

THURSDAY

How we spend our days is how we spend our lives.

—Annie Dillard

Reflection Question
- *What does this mean?*

FRIDAY

Lost time is never found again.

—Ben Franklin

Reflection Questions
- *What are some ways that you don't use your time wisely (e.g., watching too much TV, spending too much time on the phone or computer)?*

- *How could you make better use of your time?*

"CHARACTER QUOTATIONS" Tom Lickona and Matt Davidson
Kagan Publishing • 1(800) 933-2667 • www.KaganOnline.com

WORK

Without ambition, one starts nothing. Without work, one finishes nothing.

—Ralph Waldo Emerson

"CHARACTER QUOTATIONS" Tom Lickona and Matt Davidson
Kagan Publishing • 1(800) 933-2667 • www.KaganOnline.com

WORK

The harder you work, the luckier you get.

—Gary Player

"CHARACTER QUOTATIONS" **Tom Lickona and Matt Davidson**
Kagan Publishing • 1(800) 933-2667 • www.KaganOnline.com

WORK

Never put off until tomorrow what you can do today.

—Ben Franklin

"CHARACTER QUOTATIONS" Tom Lickona and Matt Davidson
Kagan Publishing • 1(800) 933-2667 • www.KaganOnline.com

WORK

How we spend our days is how we spend our lives.

—Annie Dillard

WORK

Lost time is never found again.

—Ben Franklin

"CHARACTER QUOTATIONS" Tom Lickona and Matt Davidson
Kagan Publishing • 1(800) 933-2667 • www.KaganOnline.com

WORK

“CHARACTER QUOTATIONS” Tom Lickona and Matt Davidson
Kagan Publishing • 1(800) 933-2667 • www.KaganOnline.com

KINDNESS

THE QUALITY OF BEING BENEVOLENT, CONSIDERATE, OR HELPFUL.

WEEK 31

TUESDAY

2 No act of kindness, however small, goes unnoticed.

—Aesop

Reflection Questions
- *When was a time in your life when somebody did something nice for you?*
- *Why do we remember kind acts by others?*

MONDAY

1

Goodness is the only investment that never fails.

—Henry David Thoreau

Reflection Question
- *If we are good to other people, how does that help us?*

ACTION ASSIGNMENTS

- Individually, write a letter to someone thanking that person for an act of kindness.

- As a class, discuss what makes for a good compliment (e.g., it's sincere, specific, true, is the sort of thing you'd like someone to say about you).

- From a bowl or hat containing the names of all class members, draw the name of a classmate. Sometime during the week, write an anonymous compliment about the person whose name you drew (be sure the compliment meets the class criteria for a good compliment AND don't sign your compliment). Give your anonymous compliment to the teacher, who will put it in a class compliments box. On Friday, post all the compliments on a "Compliments Bulletin Board."

WEDNESDAY

If you can't say something good about someone, don't say anything at all.

—old saying

Reflection Question
• *Why is this advice so important to follow?*

THURSDAY

Speak not a word by which anyone could be wounded.

—Hindu proverb

Reflection Question
• *If we do say words that wound someone, what can we do to heal the wound?*

FRIDAY

Be kind, for every person you meet is fighting a hard battle.

—Ian MacLaren

Reflection Question
• *What does this quote tell us?*

KINDNESS

Goodness is the only investment that never fails.

—Henry David Thoreau

Kindness

"CHARACTER QUOTATIONS" Tom Lickona and Matt Davidson
Kagan Publishing • 1(800) 933-2667 • www.KaganOnline.com

KINDNESS

No act of kindness, however small, goes unnoticed.

—Aesop

Kindness

"CHARACTER QUOTATIONS" Tom Lickona and Matt Davidson
Kagan Publishing • 1(800) 933-2667 • www.KaganOnline.com

KINDNESS

If you can't say something good about someone, don't say anything at all.

—old saying

Kindness

KINDNESS

Speak not a word by which anyone could be wounded.

—Hindu proverb

"CHARACTER QUOTATIONS" Tom Lickona and Matt Davidson
Kagan Publishing • 1(800) 933-2667 • www.KaganOnline.com

KINDNESS

Be kind, for every person you meet is fighting a hard battle.

—Ian MacLaren

Kindness

"CHARACTER QUOTATIONS" Tom Lickona and Matt Davidson
Kagan Publishing • 1(800) 933-2667 • www.KaganOnline.com

KINDNESS

"CHARACTER QUOTATIONS" Tom Lickona and Matt Davidson
Kagan Publishing • 1(800) 933-2667 • www.KaganOnline.com

JUSTICE/ FAIRNESS

TREATING PEOPLE AS THEY
DESERVE TO BE TREATED;
RESPECTING THE RIGHTS OF ALL.

WEEK 32

TUESDAY

2

Whatever is hateful to yourself, do not to your fellow man.

—**Torah**

Reflection Question
- *How can following this rule help you be a good person?*

MONDAY

1

The best indicator of our character is: (a) how we treat people who can't do us any good, and (b) how we treat people who can't fight back.

—**Dear Abby**

Reflection Question
- *How does the way we treat other people show what kind of person we are?*

ACTION ASSIGNMENTS

- Each day, keep track of the number of times you say something uncomplimentary, mean, or unfair to another person or about someone behind his or her back. Each day, make it a goal to say fewer negative things, until you no longer say them at all.

- In small groups, complete the following statements, "We can be peacemakers in our classroom by _____. We can be peacemakers in this school by _____. We can be peacemakers in our family by _____."

- As a class, make a composite list from the small group statements.

- Individually, make a plan for carrying out one of these ideas for each area— classroom, school, and home.

WEDNESDAY

If you want peace, work for justice.

—Pope Paul VI

Reflection Question
- *How can you be a peacemaker at school or at home by helping to solve a conflict fairly?*

THURSDAY

It isn't fair to ask of others what you are not willing to do yourself.

—Eleanor Roosevelt

Reflection Question
- *How do you try to do your fair share of chores in your family?*

FRIDAY

There may be times when we are powerless to prevent injustice, but there must never be a time when we fail to protest.

—Elie Wiesel

Reflection Question
- *When was a time you stood up for someone who was being treated unfairly?*

Justice / Fairness

JUSTICE/FAIRNESS

The best indicator of our character is: (a) how we treat people who can't do us any good, and (b) how we treat people who can't fight back.

—Dear Abby

JUSTICE/
FAIRNESS

Whatever is hateful to yourself, do not to your fellow man.

—Torah

"CHARACTER QUOTATIONS" **Tom Lickona and Matt Davidson**
Kagan Publishing • 1(800) 933-2667 • www.KaganOnline.com

269

JUSTICE/
FAIRNESS

If you want peace, work for justice.

—Pope Paul VI

"CHARACTER QUOTATIONS" Tom Lickona and Matt Davidson
Kagan Publishing • 1(800) 933-2667 • www.KaganOnline.com

JUSTICE/
FAIRNESS

It isn't fair to ask of others what you are not willing to do yourself.

—Eleanor Roosevelt

❝CHARACTER QUOTATIONS❞ Tom Lickona and Matt Davidson
Kagan Publishing • 1(800) 933-2667 • www.KaganOnline.com

JUSTICE/ FAIRNESS

There may be times when we are powerless to prevent injustice, but there must never be a time when we fail to protest.

—Elie Wiesel

Justice/Fairness

JUSTICE/ FAIRNESS

❝CHARACTER QUOTATIONS❞ Tom Lickona and Matt Davidson
Kagan Publishing • 1(800) 933-2667 • www.KaganOnline.com

RESPONSIBILITY

ACCOUNTABILITY FOR ONE'S
ACTIONS; DEPENDABILITY.

WEEK 33

TUESDAY

2 **The best way to give advice
is to set a good example.**
—proverb

Reflection Question
• *How do you try to set a good example for
others?*

MONDAY

1

**We create our character by
the daily decisions we make.**
—Deb Austin Brown

Reflection Question
• *How do you make a decision when you are
trying to decide what's right to do?*

ACTION ASSIGNMENTS

• At the start of each day, plan a way to
set a good example for others in your
classroom or school.

• At the end of the day, write down what
you actually did to set a good example
and one way you can do even better
tomorrow.

WEDNESDAY

He who holds the ladder is as bad as the thief.

—proverb

Reflection Question
• *What does this mean?*

THURSDAY

I am only one, but still I am one. I cannot do everything, but still I can do something.

—Edward Everett Hale

Reflection Question
• *What is one thing you could do today to make a positive difference in the life of another person?*

FRIDAY

Once you have discovered what is happening, you can't pretend not to know. Knowledge always brings responsibility.

—P. D. James

Reflection Question
• *When was a time that you felt responsible to do something once you knew what was happening?*

RESPONSIBILITY

We create our character by the daily decisions we make.

—Deb Austin Brown

"CHARACTER QUOTATIONS" Tom Lickona and Matt Davidson
Kagan Publishing • 1(800) 933-2667 • www.KaganOnline.com

RESPONSIBILITY

The best way to give advice is to set a good example.

—proverb

❝CHARACTER QUOTATIONS❞ **Tom Lickona and Matt Davidson**
Kagan Publishing • 1(800) 933-2667 • www.KaganOnline.com

RESPONSIBILITY

He who holds the ladder is as bad as the thief.

—proverb

"CHARACTER QUOTATIONS" Tom Lickona and Matt Davidson
Kagan Publishing • 1(800) 933-2667 • www.KaganOnline.com

RESPONSIBILITY

I am only one, but still I am one. I cannot do everything, but still I can do something.

—Edward Everett Hale

Responsibility

"CHARACTER QUOTATIONS" **Tom Lickona and Matt Davidson**
Kagan Publishing • 1(800) 933-2667 • www.KaganOnline.com

RESPONSIBILITY

Once you have discovered what is happening, you can't pretend not to know. Knowledge always brings responsibility.

—P. D. James

Responsibility

"CHARACTER QUOTATIONS" Tom Lickona and Matt Davidson
Kagan Publishing • 1(800) 933-2667 • www.KaganOnline.com

RESPONSIBILITY

"CHARACTER QUOTATIONS" Tom Lickona and Matt Davidson
Kagan Publishing • 1(800) 933-2667 • www.KaganOnline.com

WISDOM

GOOD JUDGMENT; KNOWLEDGE OF HOW TO LIVE LIFE WELL.

WEEK 34

TUESDAY

2

Use what talents you possess. The woods would be very quiet if no birds sang except those that sang best.

—Henry Van Dyke

Reflection Question
- *What is a way you are developing a talent you have that can bring happiness to yourself and others?*

MONDAY

1

Life is the sum of your choices.

—Albert Camus

Reflection Question
- *What can you do to help yourself make good choices in your life, starting today?*

ACTION ASSIGNMENTS

- At the start of each day, plan to do one unselfish deed in your classroom or home. At the end of the day, write about how doing this unselfish act made you feel.

- Write a paragraph about one positive choice you made during this school year and how it affected your life. Share it with a partner.

WEDNESDAY 3

Happiness begins where selfishness ends.

—John Wooden
UCLA men's basketball
coach, whose teams won a
record ten nation
championships)

Reflection Question
- *Why are we happier when we are unselfish?*

THURSDAY 4

Only a life lived for others is a life worthwhile.

—Albert Einstein

Reflection Question
- *How does helping others give meaning to your life?*

FRIDAY 5

A person wrapped up in himself makes a very small bundle.

—Ben Franklin

Reflection Question
- *What does this mean?*

"CHARACTER QUOTATIONS" Tom Lickona and Matt Davidson
Kagan Publishing • 1(800) 933-2667 • www.KaganOnline.com

WISDOM

Life is the sum of your choices.

—Albert Camus

Wisdom

WISDOM

Use what talents you possess. The woods would be very quiet if no birds sang except those that sang best.

—Henry Van Dyke

Wisdom

"CHARACTER QUOTATIONS" Tom Lickona and Matt Davidson
Kagan Publishing • 1(800) 933-2667 • www.KaganOnline.com

WISDOM

Happiness begins where selfishness ends.

—John Wooden
UCLA men's basketball coach,
whose teams won a record
ten nation championships)

Wisdom

WISDOM

Only a life lived for others is a life worthwhile.

—Albert Einstein

Wisdom

"CHARACTER QUOTATIONS" Tom Lickona and Matt Davidson
Kagan Publishing • 1(800) 933-2667 • www.KaganOnline.com

WISDOM

A person wrapped up in himself makes a very small bundle.

—Ben Franklin

"CHARACTER QUOTATIONS" Tom Lickona and Matt Davidson
Kagan Publishing • 1(800) 933-2667 • www.KaganOnline.com

WISDOM

“CHARACTER QUOTATIONS” Tom Lickona and Matt Davidson
Kagan Publishing • 1(800) 933-2667 • www.KaganOnline.com

INNER PEACE

CALMNESS OF MIND AND SPIRIT.

WEEK 35

TUESDAY

2

When I am anxious, it is because I am living in the future. When I am depressed, it is because I am living in the past.

—anonymous

Reflection Question
• *What helps us to focus on the present moment?*

MONDAY

1

Those who are free of resentful thoughts find peace.

—Buddha

Reflection Question
• *Why is this true?*

ACTION ASSIGNMENTS

• In small groups, do a RoundRobin with each person completing the following statement, "One thing I worry about is _____."

• In small groups, do a second RoundRobin completing the statement: "Something that helps me not worry so much is _____."

• Choose one new strategy to help you control worrying, and put it into practice.

What worries you, masters you.

—Haddon Robinson

Reflection Question
• *What can you say to yourself to help stop worrying about something?*

Wealth consists not of having great possessions but of having few wants.

—Epicurus

Reflection Question
• *Why is this true?*

Anyone who makes a mistake and does not admit it is making another mistake.

—Confucius

Reflection Question
• *Why does it cause more stress to deny a mistake than to admit it?*

"CHARACTER QUOTATIONS" Tom Lickona and Matt Davidson
Kagan Publishing • 1(800) 933-2667 • www.KaganOnline.com

INNER PEACE

Those who are free of resentful thoughts find peace.

—**Buddha**

Inner Peace

INNER PEACE

When I am anxious, it is because I am living in the future. When I am depressed, it is because I am living in the past.

—anonymous

"CHARACTER QUOTATIONS" Tom Lickona and Matt Davidson
Kagan Publishing • 1(800) 933-2667 • www.KaganOnline.com

293

INNER
PEACE

What worries you, masters you.

—Haddon Robinson

Inner Peace

"CHARACTER QUOTATIONS" Tom Lickona and Matt Davidson
Kagan Publishing • 1(800) 933-2667 • www.KaganOnline.com

INNER PEACE

Wealth consists not of having great possessions but of having few wants.

—Epicurus

"CHARACTER QUOTATIONS" Tom Lickona and Matt Davidson
Kagan Publishing • 1(800) 933-2667 • www.KaganOnline.com

INNER PEACE

Anyone who makes a mistake and does not admit it is making another mistake.

—Confucius

Inner Peace

"CHARACTER QUOTATIONS" Tom Lickona and Matt Davidson
Kagan Publishing • 1(800) 933-2667 • www.KaganOnline.com

INNER PEACE

"CHARACTER QUOTATIONS" Tom Lickona and Matt Davidson
Kagan Publishing • 1(800) 933-2667 • www.KaganOnline.com

WISDOM

GOOD JUDGMENT; KNOWLEDGE
OF HOW TO LIVE LIFE WELL.

WEEK 36

TUESDAY

2

If you do not have the time to do it right, when will you find the time to do it over?

—**John Wooden**
UCLA men's basketball coach, whose teams won a record ten nation championships)

Reflection Question
• *How could this saying help you?*

MONDAY

No one makes a greater mistake than the person who does nothing because he could do only a little.

—**Edmund Burke**

Reflection Question
• *Why is it a mistake to do nothing because you think you can only do a little?*

ACTION ASSIGNMENTS

• Choose one of your favorite quotes from this year. Send a card to someone who is important to you, including this quote as part of your message.

• Write a positive note to a teacher, peer, or adult in your family. In your note, tell something about that person that you appreciate or admire.

WEDNESDAY

Better safe than sorry.
—proverb

Reflection Question
• *What does this mean?*

THURSDAY

Nonviolence is the weapon of the strong.
—Mahatma Gandhi

Reflection Question
• *How does it show strength to refrain from violence?*

FRIDAY

Words go into the body.
—Maya Angelou

Reflection Questions
• *What does this mean?*

• *Have you experienced this?*

Wisdom

WISDOM

No one makes a greater mistake than the person who does nothing because he could do only a little.

—Edmund Burke

Wisdom

WISDOM

If you do not have the time to do it right, when will you find the time to do it over?

—John Wooden
UCLA men's basketball coach, whose teams won a record ten nation championships)

"CHARACTER QUOTATIONS" **Tom Lickona and Matt Davidson**
Kagan Publishing • 1(800) 933-2667 • www.KaganOnline.com

WISDOM

Better safe than sorry.

—proverb

"CHARACTER QUOTATIONS" Tom Lickona and Matt Davidson
Kagan Publishing • 1(800) 933-2667 • www.KaganOnline.com

WISDOM

Nonviolence is the weapon of the strong.

—Mahatma Gandhi

Wisdom

❝CHARACTER QUOTATIONS❞ Tom Lickona and Matt Davidson
Kagan Publishing • 1(800) 933-2667 • www.KaganOnline.com

WISDOM

Words go into the body.

—Maya Angelou

Wisdom

"CHARACTER QUOTATIONS" Tom Lickona and Matt Davidson
Kagan Publishing • 1(800) 933-2667 • www.KaganOnline.com

WISDOM

"CHARACTER QUOTATIONS" Tom Lickona and Matt Davidson
Kagan Publishing • 1(800) 933-2667 • www.KaganOnline.com

CHARACTER EDUCATION
RESOURCES

Beedy, J.P., (1997). *Sports PLUS (Positive Learning Using Sports): Developing youth sports programs that teach positive values.* Hamilton, MA: Project Adventure, Inc.
www.sportsplus.org

Beedy, J.P., & Davidson, M.L. (in press) *GoodSport Youth Development Program: A sport, literacy, and character development program.* New Hampton, NH: New Hampton School.
www.sportsplus.org

Borba, M., (2001). *Building moral intelligence: The seven essential virtues that teach kids to do the right thing.* San Francisco: Jossey-Bass.

Borba, M., (2003). *No more misbehavin': 38 difficult behaviors and how to stop them.*
San Francisco: Jossey-Bass.

"Creating caring schools." (March, 2003). *Educational Leadership.*

Developmental Studies Center, (1996). *Ways we want our class to be: Class meetings that build commitment to kindness and learning.* Oakland, CA: Developmental Studies Center.
www.devstu.org

The Fourth and Fifth Rs. Newsletter of the Center for the 4th and 5th Rs
www.cortland.edu/c4n5rs

Gauld, J.W., (1993). *Character first: The Hyde School difference.* San Francisco: Institute for Contemporary Studies.

Gauld, L. & M., (2002). *The biggest job we'll ever have: The Hyde School Program for Character-Based Education and Parenting.* New York: Scribner.

Heartwood Ethics Curriculum: An ethics curriculum for children. Pittsburgh: Heartwood Ethics Institute. **www.heartwoodethics.org**

Josephson, M.J., (2001). *You don't have to be sick to get better: Thoughts on being a better person and living a better life.* Marina del Rey, CA: Josephson Institute of Ethics.
www.charactercounts.org

Journal of Research on Character Education.
www.baylor.edu/~Andrew_Milson/jrce.html

Kagan, S., (1992). *Cooperative learning.* San Clemente, CA: Kagan Publishing.
www.KaganOnline.com

306

❝**CHARACTER QUOTATIONS**❞ **Tom Lickona and Matt Davidson**
Kagan Publishing • 1(800) 933-2667 • www.KaganOnline.com

Kaminsky, M., (2000). *Uncommon Champions: Fifteen athletes who battled back.* Honesdale, PA: Boyds Mills Press.

Kilpatrick, W., Wolfe, G., & Wolfe, S., (1994). *Books that build character: A guide to teaching your child moral values through stories.* New York: Touchstone.

Klee, M.B., (2000). *Core virtues: A literature-based program in character education.* Redwood City, CA: The Link Institute. **www.linkinstitute.org**

Kolomeisky, D., (2001). *All about you: A course in character for teens.* Gaithersburg, MD: The Whole Person Project.

Lickona, T., (2004). *Character matters: How to help our children develop good judgment, integrity, and other essential virtues.* New York: Simon and Schuster.

Lickona, T., (2003). "Talking to kids about sex, love, and character." **www.cortland.edu/c4n5rs**

Lickona, T., (1991). *Educating for character: How our schools can teach respect and responsibility.* New York: Bantam Books.

Lickona, T., (1983). *Raising good children: From birth through the teenage years.* New York: Bantam Books.

McAdam, C.C., McAdam, R., & Bange, D., (2001). *Portraits of character: Books I and II.* San Clemente, CA: Kagan Publishing. **www.KaganOnline.com**

Murphy, M.M., (2002). *Character education in America's Blue Ribbon Schools: Best practices for meeting the challenge.* Maryland: Scarecrow Press, Inc.

National Schools of Character and Promising Practices Citations. (published each year based on an annual awards competition). Washington, DC: Character Education Partnership. **www.character.org**

Posey, J., & Davidson, M.L., (2001). *Character education evaluation toolkit: A user-friendly and practical evaluation guide for educators and administrators.* Washington, DC: Character Education Partnership. **www.character.orgs**

Ryan, K., & Bohlin, K. (1999). *Building character in schools: Practical ways to bring moral instruction to life.* San Francisco: Jossey-Bass.

Shaw, V. (1992). *Communitybuilding in the classroom.* San Clemente, CA: Kagan Publishing. **www.KaganOnline.com**

Vincent, P. (1999). *Promising practices in character education: 12 success stories from around the country, Vols. 1 and 2.* Chapel Hill, NC: Character Development Publishing. **www.CharacterEducation.com**

For a more complete list of character education resources, please visit the website of the Center for the 4th and 5th Rs:
www.cortland.edu/c4n5rs

Acknowledgements

We would like to thank Spencer Kagan for inviting us to do a book on character quotes and for his thoughtful suggestions about content.

We are grateful to Miguel Kagan for his creative work on the book's design and for his chapter on cooperative structures that engage students in discussing the quotes, the weekly virtues, and the concept of character.

We appreciate the helpful editorial suggestions of Marthe Seales, administrative assistant at our Center for the 4th and 5th Rs.

We appreciate Alex Core's terrific work on the book layout and cover design and coloring. We appreciate the cover illustration by Celso Rodriguez.

We are grateful to Kimberly Fields for copyediting the book and her many helpful corrections.

Finally, we are indebted to the quotation authors, without whose wisdom we would all be poorer.

"CHARACTER QUOTATIONS" **Tom Lickona and Matt Davidson**
Kagan Publishing • 1(800) 933-2667 • www.KaganOnline.com

Notes

NOTES

"CHARACTER QUOTATIONS" Tom Lickona and Matt Davidson
Kagan Publishing • 1(800) 933-2667 • www.KaganOnline.com

NOTES

NOTES

NOTES

NOTES